I Am You

Cookbook by Trang Moreland

I Am You - Cookbook by Trang Moreland

Copyright © 2024 by Trang Moreland. All rights reserved.

No part of this publication may be reproduced by photocopying, scanning, or any other means, or stored in a retrieval system, or transmitted in any form, or published by any means, without prior written permission of the author, except in the case of brief quotations embodied in critical articles and reviews.

ISBN 979-8-218-32396-7

Cover Design by Melissa Moreland.

Introduction

Everyone loves to cook, right? Or so I thought.

It amazes me how many people (including my husband) I've heard say, "I hate to cook!" I never heard such a thing while growing up in Viet Nam. My mom always kept the kids around when she was preparing food. Thanks to her, I learned to appreciate cooking at a very young age.

Cooking was very different for us. We caught our own fish from the river; we gathered vegetables from the garden we planted and tended ourselves; then, we built fires to cook over since we had no electricity.

When I first came to America at the age of 21, I was amazed how easy cooking could be! Just a turn of a dial on the stove and, voilà, instant fire! Plus, I had a sink with running water and a roll of paper towels hanging nearby. What more could I ask for!

When I made steamed rice for my husband, he told me he'd only ever had rice made with milk and sugar. I decided then that I needed to learn some American-style meals as well.

Our children, Rick and Melissa, loved both types of cuisine. Along with my in-laws, they had a difficult time deciding what I should make for our family dinners. Often times, it resulted in me making two different meals at once!

Our children went on to start their own lives, taking with them much of my cooking know-how. Rick lives nearby, while Melissa has moved to New York City. Both greatly enjoy cooking.

I remember the time Melissa texted me a picture of a meal she was preparing. I smiled and typed back, "I can't believe you still eat just like me!" To this, she replied, "I am you!" I laughed and cried at the same time. It truly was one of the happiest moments of my life!

The words "I am you" stuck in my head; meanwhile, thoughts of writing a cookbook slowly crept into my mind. Not only could I preserve my recipes for my children, but I could also share them with so many others. Many ideas came and went over the next three years, but one thing remained certain: the name of my cookbook would be "I Am You."

The recipes I'm sharing with you are an unusual combination of Vietnamese and American cuisine. For over 30 years, I have frequently prepared each of these meals for both my family and for thousands of customers who dined at my formerly owned family-style restaurant.

I've spent countless hours making these recipes easy to understand, simple to make, yet as flavorful and healthy as possible.

I'm so happy you have found this book. My hope is that you'll enjoy cooking these dishes and come to love their taste and diversity, even if you are someone who once said, "I hate to cook!"

Much Love
Trang Moreland

Acknowledgments

Cooking has always come easily to me, but transferring my dishes to paper has taken years of hard work and help from many different sources.

The idea for this book would never have been born without the inspiring influence of my sweet daughter, Melissa, the constant feedback from my awesome son, Rick, and my amazing husband, who has patiently worked by my side.

A very big thank you to my brilliant editor, Cherie Kail, for all her edits, recipe feedback, and for remaining my friend all these years.

I would also like to thank the following people and businesses: Jim Gill and Staff at the Dover Public Library; Ashley Spears and all the vendors of the Walnut Creek Amish Flea Market; my Amish friend, Cindy Raber; my Aunt Lien and niece, Quyen; and the many other special people who sampled the recipes and provided feedback.

There are no words that can describe the immense respect I have for my mother. Not only did she teach me to cook at a very young age, but more importantly, she instilled in me the qualities of kindness and working hard.

I want to give special thanks to all my family and friends for their never ending love, support, and encouragement.

And to all the readers of my first book, Just Smile and Say Hello, I sincerely thank you for extending your support into my next project.

Lastly, I am forever grateful to everyone who pre-ordered I Am You. Your confidence in me has allowed me to bring this cookbook from my dreams to reality.

Table of Contents

Cooking Rice VI

Don't Skip The MSG VII

Chicken Curry 1

Chicken Stir Fry 5

Hamburger Fried Rice 7

Bitter Melon With Egg 9

Banh Xeo 11

Sweet and Salty Pork Chops 15

Chicken Fried Rice 17

Shrimp Fried Rice 19

Egg Rolls 21

Gourd or Chayote Soup 25

Green Papaya Salad 27

Okra and Hamburger With Rice 29

Rice Noodles With Cabbage 31

Pepper Steak Stir Fry 33

Pork and Fish Sauce With Rice 35

Bitter Melon Soup With Meat Balls 37

Fresh Spring Rolls 41

Steak and Mustard Greens 43

Fried Fish With Vietnamese Sauce 45

Rice Soup With Chicken & Mushrooms . 47

Meatloaf 49

Amish Noodles 51

Lasagna 53

Sweet and Spicy Fish Sauce 55

Peanut Butter & Hoisin Sauce 56

Crispy Shredded Sweet Potato 57

Sautéed Shrimp 58

Crispy Tofu 59

Boiled and Sliced Pork 61

Sweet & Sour Kohlrabi & Carrots 63

Vietnamese Sweet Rice & Bean Desert . . 65

Sweet Rice and Mung Beans 67

Cooking Rice

Rice has always been my best friend, starting from the time I was old enough to eat solid foods. In Viet Nam, we ate rice three times a day, every day, and it was always cooked over an open fire made with sticks and straw.

I watched my mom for many years use her index finger and eyes to gauge the correct amount of water when cooking rice. I grew up learning to do the same. One look and we can tell exactly if it's the right amount of water. Over the years, your eyes become trained and you just know. My American husband is still amazed at what he jokingly refers to as our "Asian eyes".

After coming to live in America, I began using a rice cooker. Alongside using a measuring cup, it consistently made perfectly cooked rice. As a busy mom, it's great to hit a button, walk away to do house work or run errands, and return to a pot of ready-to-eat rice. Even though I've burnt rice more times than I can count when cooking over a fire, my memory keeps telling me the rice always tasted better.

Preparations

Rinsing rice before cooking is an important step that shouldn't be skipped. It removes excess starch and any dust or unwanted debris.

Measure the desired amount of rice into cooker pot and cover with water. Swish rice around with your hand until water becomes cloudy. Drain off water and repeat 2 to 3 times or until water remains fairly clear. After final rinse, drain off as much water as possible.

For choosing the right amount of water when using a rice cooker, the table below shows the ratios that have worked best for me. For those who prefer using an instant pot or cooking on stovetop, I recommend consulting reliable online sources.

Long-Grain White Rice
1 cup uncooked rice - use 1¼ cups water = 2¾ cups cooked rice
1½ cups uncooked rice - use 1½ cups water = 4¼ cups cooked rice
3 cups uncooked rice - use 2½ cups water = 8¼ cups cooked rice

Long-Grain Brown Rice
1 cup uncooked rice - use 2 cups water = 3 cups cooked rice
1½ cups uncooked rice - use 2¾ cups water = 4¼ cups cooked rice
3 cups uncooked rice - use 4 cups water = 8¼ cups cooked rice

Cooking

1. Add proper amount of water, making sure rice is evenly spread on bottom of pot.
2. Follow manufacturer instructions for cooker operation.
3. Allow rice to rest for 15 minutes after cooking for best results.
4. Stir and enjoy!!!

Don't Skip The MSG

You will find MSG listed as an ingrediant in many of these recipes. Some people may be worried about using it. Leaving out the MSG won't greatly change the end result of most of the dishes; however, omiting MSG from egg rolls, stir fries, fried rice, bitter melon dishes, okra, and rice noodles with cabbage will result in a very bland dish. MSG is necessary in these recipes to enhance the flavor and make sure your food is the tastiest it can be.

What exactly is MSG

MSG, a naturally occurring compound in tomatoes, cheese, mushrooms, and various other foods, is a common additive found in canned vegetables, ketchup, mustard, deli meats, potato chips, and soups.

The packaged MSG available in stores is produced by fermenting corn, sugar cane, sugar beets, tapioca, or molasses. It's the purest form of "umami" (pronounced oo-mah-mee), one of the five taste sensations alongside sweet, sour, bitter, and salty. MSG, short for monosodium glutamate, is the sodium salt of glutamic acid. Remarkably, it contains two-thirds less sodium than regular table salt.

Despite its presence in numerous everyday foods, MSG faced unwarranted skepticism in the late 1960s, owing to unfounded claims and unreliable scientific studies. Since then, global regulatory bodies have endorsed MSG as safe for consumption, supported by a lack of hard evidence linking it to health conditions. Notably, many popular food items containing MSG, such as Doritos, Kraft Mac & Cheese, Campbell's Cream of Mushroom Soup, or Lipton Soup mix, generally do not cause reported headaches or adverse reactions.

Using MSG offers the added advantage of reducing sodium intake while increasing the savory flavor of your meals. As a seasoning, it takes your favorite dishes to the next level, making it a valuable addition to your kitchen.

AROY-D
COCONUT MILK
NET CONTENTS

S&B®
ORIENTAL
CURRY
POWDER
特製エスビーカレー
ngredients: Turmeric, Coriander, Fenugreek,
umin, Orange Peel, Pepper, Chili Pepper,
nnamon, Fennel, Ginger, Star Anise, Thyme,
ay Leaves, Cloves, Nutmeg, Sage, Cardamom

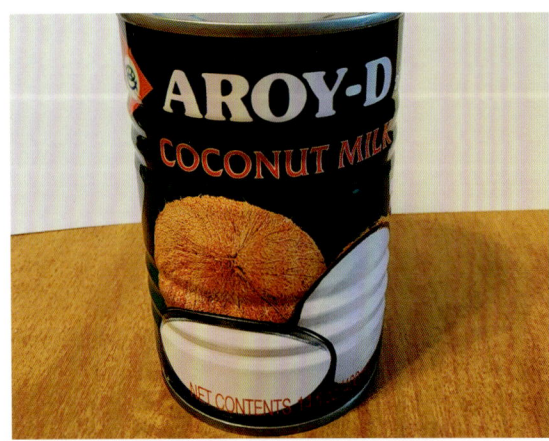

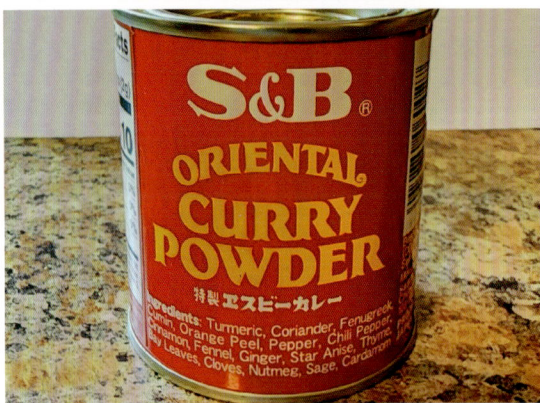

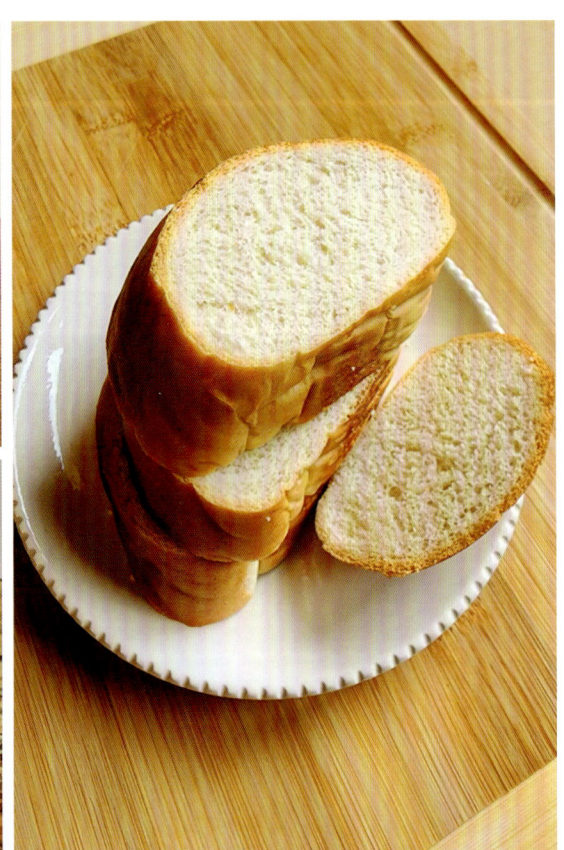

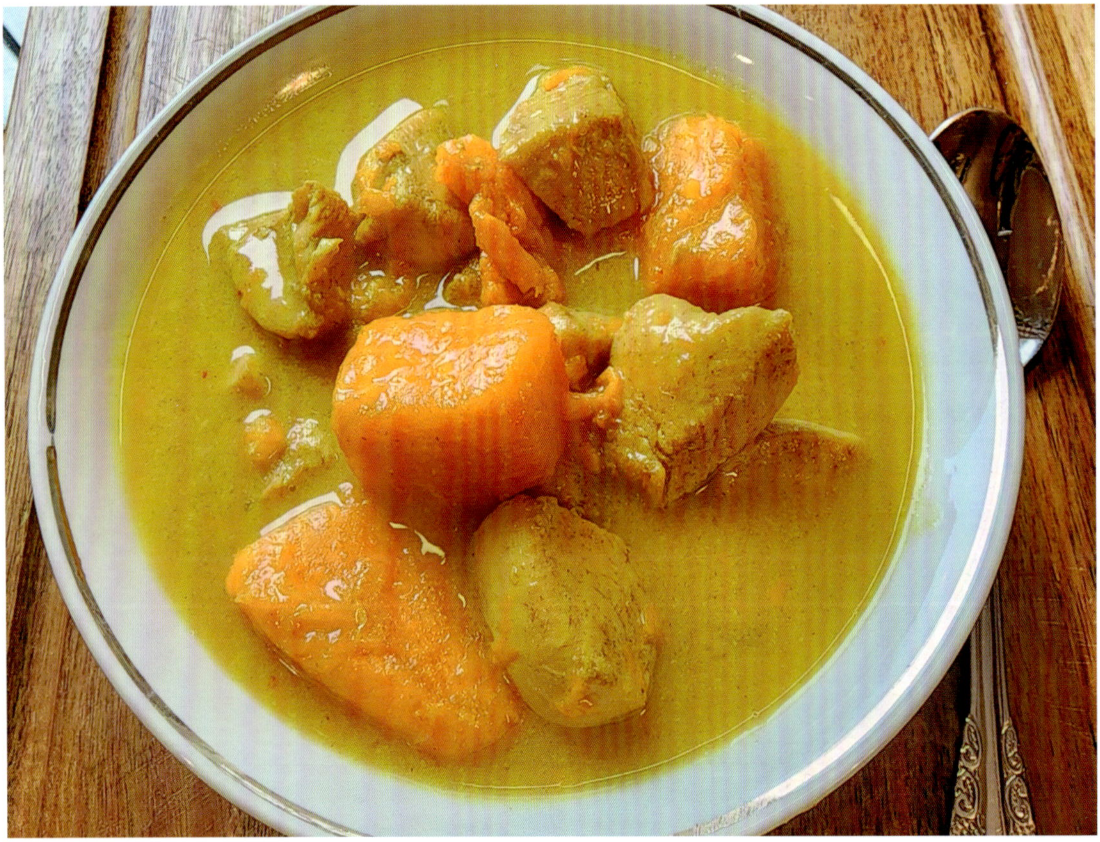

Chicken Curry

2 lbs. Boneless skinless chicken
Turmeric powder
Curry power
Salt
MSG
2½ lbs. Sweet potatoes
Olive oil
¾ cup sliced yellow onion

2 cups chicken broth
Sugar
2 slices ginger
1 hot chili pepper (finely chopped)
1 cup milk
1 can (13½ oz.) coconut milk
Corn starch
1 loaf French bread.

1. Cut chicken into bite size pieces and place in medium size bowl. Add ¼ teaspoon turmeric powder, 2 teaspoons curry powder, 1 teaspoon salt, and 1 teaspoon MSG. Mix well and allow to sit 30 minutes.

Note: To insure intended flavor of this dish, choose curry powder that includes the additional ingredients - Ginger and Anise Seed.

2. Peel and clean sweet potatoes, cut each one into 1½ inch sections then cut each section into 4 pieces. Soak potatoes in water to prevent browning and drain well before cooking.

3. In large skillet, add 2 tablespoons olive oil and place over medium heat. Add ¾ cup sliced yellow onion and stir until onions begin turning brown. Add seasoned chicken and stir constantly for 4 minutes. Remove from heat, set aside.

4. In 4 or 6 quart sauce pan, add 2 cups water, 2 cups chicken broth, ½ tablespoon sugar, ½ teaspoon salt, ½ teaspoon turmeric powder, and 2 small slices ginger. Bring to a boil then add contents of skillet with chicken. Cook with a low boil for 10 minutes, stirring occasionally.

5. Add sweet potatoes and 1 cup milk, bring back to boil. Continue with low boil for 5 minutes, stirring occasionally.

Continued next page →

Serves 4 - 6

Chicken Curry (continued)

6. Add 1 can coconut milk, 2 tablespoons sugar, ½ teaspoon salt, and 2 teaspoons curry powder. Bring back to a low boil and continue cooking for an additional 12 minutes while stirring occasionally.

7. In small bowl, combine 2 tablespoons corn starch with 2 tablespoons water and mix well. Add corn starch mixture to sauce pan and 1 finely chopped hot chili pepper. Simmer for 12 minutes, stirring occasionally. Remove from heat and allow to sit with no cover for 15-20 minutes. Serve and enjoy!

Note: Refrigerate leftovers after allowing to cool. This dish is supposed to taste sweet, salty, and spicy all at the same time. To avoid changing its unique flavor, please don't skip or cut back on any seasoning.

Best when eaten with a piece of French bread broken off by hand and dipped in the sauce, and using fork or chopsticks for the rest. This dish is also great served on top of rice or fresh rice noodles.

In Viet Nam, my family always used fresh lemon grass in this dish, but it's not easy to find in Ohio. If you would like to try adding lemon grass, just use about 3 stalks. Remove 1 inch of stalk from root end and peel off any dead layers. Cut stalk into 2½ inch lengths and lightly smack to break fibers. The lemon grass used in this dish is mainly for flavoring and should be finely chopped before deciding to eat.

Chicken Stir Fry

3 cups cooked rice

1½ tablespoons butter

½ cup sliced yellow onion

8 oz. sliced boneless chicken

Salt, MSG

1 teaspoon dark soy sauce

1¼ cups sliced broccoli

½ cup sliced carrots

Corn starch

Snow Peas (optional)

1. Begin by cooking white or brown rice.

2. In large skillet, add 1½ tablespoons butter and ½ cup sliced onion. Place over medium heat and stir until onions turn golden brown. Remove from heat. Add 8 oz. sliced chicken, ¼ teaspoon salt, ¼ teaspoon MSG, and 1 teaspoon dark soy sauce.

3. Place over high heat and continue stirring nonstop for 3 minutes or until the chicken is mostly cooked.

4. Add 2 cups water, 1¼ cups sliced broccoli, ¼ cup sliced carrots, ¼ teaspoon salt and ¼ teaspoon MSG. Allow to boil for 6 minutes until chicken is done. Add snow peas (optional).

5. In a small bowl, add 2 tablespoons corn starch and ¼ cup cool water. Mix well. Pour bowl mixture slowly into the stir fry while continuing to stir for 1-3 minutes, depending on how well you like your broccoli done.

6. If you prefer a thinner gravy, use less of the corn starch mixture. If the gravy happens to be too thick, add more water. Taste and add salt if needed. Remove from heat and serve over rice. Best when eaten with an egg roll on the side. Enjoy!

Note: This dish was always my best seller when I owned a restaurant. Many people enjoy it with soy sauce and/or sriracha hot chili sauce. Feel free to exchange the broccoli with Napa cabbage. Many of my dishes are prepared with extra virgin olive oil, but this one, I highly recommend cooking with butter.

Serves 3

Hamburger Fried Rice

3½ cups cooked rice
8 oz. ground beef (75/25)
Salt
MSG
Black pepper
⅓ cup chopped yellow onions

1 cup thin sliced green cabbage
⅓ cup shredded carrots
2 tablespoons chicken broth
1 egg
Dark soy sauce
2 chopped green onions (optional)

1. Cook white or brown rice and allow to cool to room temperature before frying. Hot rice tends to remain stuck together when frying.

2. In small bowl, add 8 oz. ground beef, ⅛ teaspoon salt, ¼ teaspoon MSG, and a touch of black pepper. Mix well.

3. In large skillet, add seasoned ground beef and ⅓ cup chopped yellow onions. Place over high heat and stir for 3-4 minutes or until ground beef is done. Remove from heat, transfer skillet contents into small bowl.

4. Drain grease from bowl with cooked ground beef into small container. Add 3 tablespoons of grease from container back into skillet. If using leaner meat and don't have enough grease, use olive oil as substitute.

5. Add 3½ cups cooked rice and 1 cup sliced green cabbage to skillet, place over high heat. Stir for 2 minutes and remove from heat.

6. Add cooked ground beef from bowl, ⅓ cup shredded carrots, 2 tablespoons chicken broth, ½ teaspoon MSG, 1 egg (lightly beaten), and 2 teaspoons dark soy sauce.

7. Place back over high heat and stir for 5 minutes or until cooked to your liking. Remove from heat, mix in chopped green onions (optional), serve and enjoy!

Note: Most enjoy eating this dish with soy sauce and/or sriracha hot chili sauce. My husband prefers Sweet and Spicy Fish Sauce With Carrots (page 55).

Serves 3

Bitter Melon with Egg

- 2 cups cooked rice
- 2 cups or 1 bitter melon (thin sliced)
- 4 eggs
- Fish sauce
- MSG
- Black pepper
- Olive oil
- 2 cloves garlic (chopped)
- 1 green onion (chopped)
- Salt
- Sugar

1. Cook white or brown rice and have ready.

2. Thoroughly wash bitter melon, cut off both ends and cut melon in half lengthwise. Use a teaspoon to scrape and remove all seeds before slicing thin.

3. In bowl, add 4 eggs, ½ teaspoon fish sauce, ¼ teaspoon MSG, and touch of black pepper. Mix while lightly beating eggs.

4. In skillet, add 1½ tablespoons olive oil and 2 chopped garlic cloves. Place over medium heat and stir until garlic begins to brown, remove from heat.

5. Add sliced bitter melon, 1 chopped green onion, ¼ teaspoon salt, ¼ teaspoon MSG, and ½ teaspoon sugar. Place back over medium heat, stir for 2 minutes.

6. Add ¼ cup water and cook while constantly stirring until water is mostly evaporated (2 minutes).

7. Add contents of bowl with eggs, cook for 1 minute while slowly stirring to allow eggs to bond with bitter melon. After bonding occurs, continue cooking approximately 2 minutes or until eggs are lightly brown; turn 2-3 times to prevent burning. Remove from heat, enjoy!

Note: This dish is served with rice, fish sauce, or soy sauce. My husband didn't like the taste at first, but now he loves it. Dipping bitter melon in fish sauce before eating with a little rice gives it a unique flavor and makes the bitter taste less noticeable. Bitter melon is a rich source of vitamins A, C, and folic acid, and is believed to offer many health benefits..

Serves 2

Banh Xeo (Vietnamese Crepe)

1 cup peeled yellow mung beans
Salt
Sweet and spicy fish sauce (page 55)
14.1 oz. package rice flour (Banh Xeo)
14 oz. coconut milk
2 chopped green onions

Olive oil
1 lb. pork belly sliced (page 61) or 12 oz. cooked shrimp.
1 lb. bean sprouts
Leaf lettuce
Mint and Basil (optional)

1. Soak 1 cup peeled yellow mung beans in warm water for 1 hour. Rinse well.

2. In medium sauce pan, add soaked mung beans, 3 cups water, and ¼ teaspoon salt. Bring to boil then reduce to a simmer. Cook for 5 minutes or until tender but not mushy. Drain well and set aside uncovered.

3. Prepare sweet and spicy fish sauce (page 55)

4. In large bowl, add 14.1 oz. package rice flour (Banh Xeo) and small bag of turmeric included inside flour package. Add 14 oz. can of coconut milk, 14 oz. water, 2 chopped green onions, and ½ teaspoon salt. Mix well.

5. Using a small sauce bowl, add 2 tablespoons olive oil then lightly coat large skillet bottom with basting brush.

6. Preheat skillet over medium heat then pour ½ cup of the Banh Xeo mix into the middle of skillet. Wait a few seconds to allow batter to begin to stick, then tilt and rotate skillet to evenly spread batter.

7. Quickly add desired amount of mung beans, sliced pork belly or thawed cooked shrimp, and bean sprouts onto half of the Banh Xeo, just like you would with an omelet.

8. Cover and fry for 2 minutes, then uncover to allow steam to escape which helps make the batter crisp. Wait until the edges start to curl then brush on a little more oil around the edges of skillet.

9. Lift up the batter, checking if it's cooked to your liking, then fold in half just like you would with an omelet. Remove from skillet, place on plate. Repeat steps 5-9 for more Banh Xeo. Serve and enjoy!

Continued next page →

Makes 8-10 Banh Xeo

Banh Xeo (continued)

Note: Leftover batter can be refrigerated and kept for a few days. Banh xeo is best eaten while still hot and crispy and served with sweet and spicy fish sauce. It's intended to be eaten with your hands by taking a leaf of lettuce, adding a piece of cooked Banh Xeo, a leaf of basil, mint, then wrapping it up and dipping in sweet and spicy fish sauce.

My husband doesn't like to wrap, so he adds everything in a bowl and pours a little sweet and spicy fish sauce on top before eating with a fork. He also doesn't like mint or basil and eats it with lettuce only. It's a fun dish to share with family and friends.

Tip for selecting fresh bean sprouts

Snap a couple of sprouts in two. Good bean sprouts will be crispy, but old spouts will be limp and taste like dirt. Most bean sprouts sold at Asian markets are in an open container and most of the time are good. Other sprouts are sold in sealed bags like the ones you'll usually find at your local grocery store. They look good to the eye but can't be tested.

The best way to always have fresh bean sprouts is to grow your own. I've tried different methods of growing them and by far the best results have been with using a Bean Sprout Machine like the one pictured. They're not overly expensive and can be purchased online.

Sweet & Salty Pork Chops

Fish sauce

MSG

Honey

3 pork chops (thin)

Olive oil

2 cloves garlic (chopped)

3 cups cooked rice

1. Cook white or brown rice and have ready.

2. Tenderize 3 thin pork chops using the back of a knife or a meat tenderizer.

3. In large bowl, add 2 **tablespoons** fish sauce and ½ teaspoon MSG, stir for 1 minute. Add 1 **tablespoon** honey, mix well. Add tenderized pork chops and thoroughly cover with fish sauce and honey mix. Allow to marinate for 30 minutes.

4. In skillet, add 1 **tablespoon** olive oil, 2 cloves chopped garlic, then place over medium heat. Add marinated pork chops as soon as the skillet is hot, stir and turn for 3 minutes or until they begin to brown.

5. Add ⅓ cup water, cover skillet and occasionally stir and turn for 3 minutes. Uncover skillet, stir and turn for 2 minutes.

6. Apply 2 **tablespoons** honey over pork chops and constantly stir and turn until liquid caramelizes. Remove from heat, serve with rice and enjoy!

Note: This dish is also great with cucumbers, fried zucchini, and fish sauce or soy sauce. Pork chops will already be a little salty so use fish sauce in small bowl for dipping vegetables.

When I was young, pork chops were never within our family's budget. Now, my mother makes this dish whenever we go back to visit. My husband and kids love it constantly ask me to make it. They say mine is almost as good as Mom's.

Make sure to open a window while cooking this dish. The smell from the heated fish sauce will be a little strong.

Serves 3

Chicken Fried Rice

3½ cups cooked rice
8oz. Boneless chicken breast
                (Sliced thin)
MSG, Salt, Black pepper
Butter
Yellow onion (sliced)
1 cup broccoli (sliced)

⅓ cup carrots (sliced)
Soy sauce
Dark soy sauce
1 egg
Olive oil
1-2 chopped green onions

1. Cook white or brown rice and allow to cool to room temperature before frying. Hot rice tends to remain stuck together when frying.

2. In medium size bowl, add sliced chicken, ¼ teaspoon MSG, ⅛ teaspoon salt, and sprinkle of black pepper. Mix and set aside.

3. In large skillet, add 1 tablespoon butter and ¼ cup sliced yellow onions. Place over high heat and stir until butter melts.

4. Add chicken and stir for 2½ minutes. Add sliced broccoli and sliced carrots. Stir for 2 minutes, remove from heat. Add 1 teaspoon soy sauce and 2 tablespoons water. Place back over high heat and continue stirring for 2 more minutes or until chicken is done. Remove from heat, transfer skillet contents to medium size bowl.

5. Wipe skillet with paper towel, then add 1 tablespoon butter and ¼ cup sliced yellow onion. Place over high heat and stir until butter melts. Add 3½ cups cooked rice and stir for 2 minutes. Remove from heat.

6. Add contents of bowl with chicken and vegetables, ½ teaspoon MSG, 1 teaspoon dark soy sauce, 2 tablespoons soy sauce, 1 egg (lightly beaten), and 2 tablespoons water. Place over high heat and constantly stir for 3 minutes. Add 1 tablespoon olive oil, stir for 1 minute and remove from heat. Mix in chopped green onions, serve and enjoy!

Note: Cooking this dish takes me back to the time I owned a restaurant. It was one of the most popular dishes, quick to cook and my customers loved it. Most of them enjoyed eating it with egg rolls (page21), soy sauce and/or sriracha hot chili sauce.

Serves 3

Shrimp Fried Rice

3½ cups cooked rice
8 oz. cooked shrimp (med. size)
Salt
MSG
Black pepper
Butter

⅓ cup chopped yellow onions
Soy sauce
Dark soy sauce
1 egg
Olive oil
2 chopped green onions

1. Cook white or brown rice and allow to cool to room temperature before frying. Hot rice tends to remain stuck together when frying.

2. In a bowl, add 8 oz. cooked shrimp (make sure shrimp is thawed, clean, and free of water), ¼ teaspoon salt, ½ teaspoon MSG, and sprinkle of black pepper. Toss well and set aside.

3. In large skillet, add 1 tablespoon butter and ⅓ cup chopped yellow onion. Place over high heat and stir until butter melts.

4. Add shrimp bowl and continue cooking over high heat, stirring for 2 minutes. Add 1 more tablespoon butter, stir for 1 minute, remove from heat.

5. Add 3½ cups cooked rice, ¼ teaspoon MSG, 1 tablespoon soy sauce, 1 teaspoon dark soy sauce, and 1 egg (lightly beaten). Place back over high heat, stir for 3 minutes, add 1 tablespoon olive oil and stir for 1 more minute. Remove from heat, mix in 2 chopped green onions, serve and enjoy!

Note: This dish is great served with cucumbers, pineapple, your favorite hot pepper, soy sauce, or Sweet and Spicy Fish Sauce With Carrots (page 55).

Serves 3

BÁNH TRÁNG
EXTRA THIN
RICE PAPER
CÔ GÁI VIỆT NAM
DOUBLE PARROT
HƯƠNG VỊ QUÊ NHÀ
INGREDIENTS : RICE FLOUR, TAPIOCA FLOUR, SALT, WATER.
SPRING ROLL WRAPPER
NET WT : 20 OZ (570G)
Distributor : IHA BEVERAGE
COMMERCE, CA 90040
PRODUCT OF VIETNAM

FARBERWARE

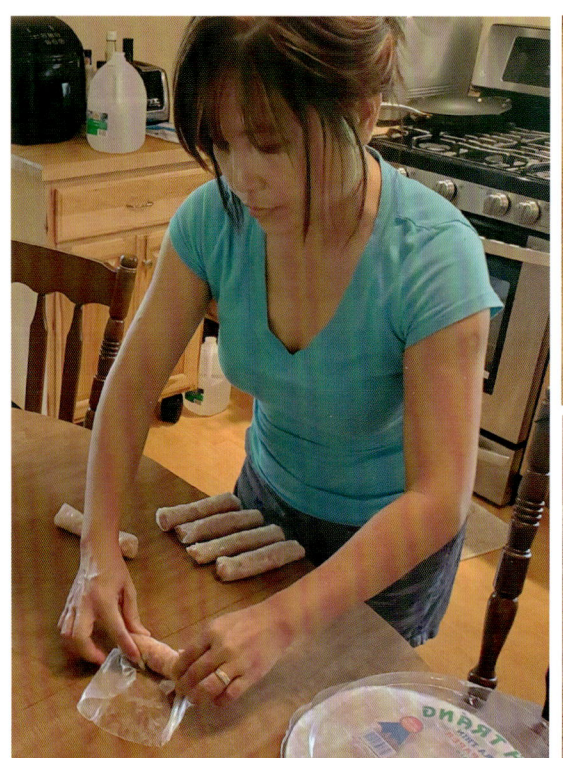

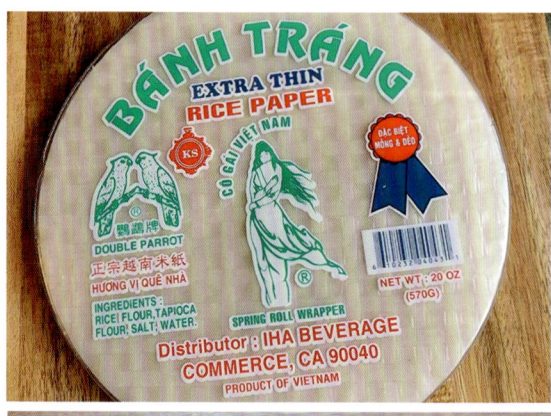

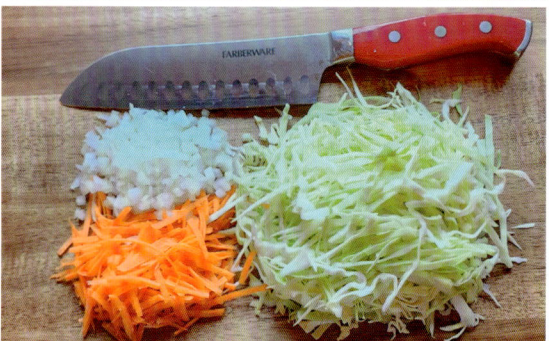

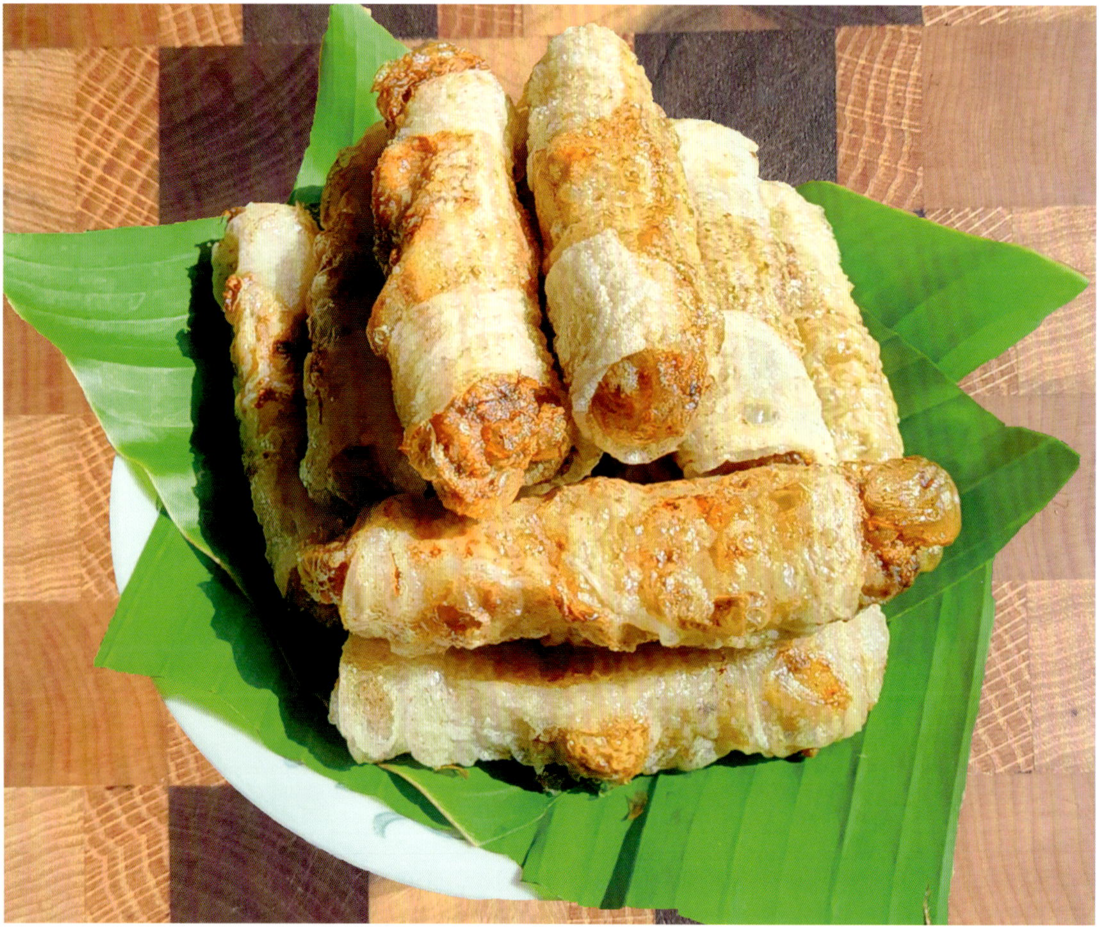

Egg Rolls

1 package rice paper (9¾ inch)
1 lb. unseasoned ground chicken or ground pork
Salt, MSG, Paprika
2 cups green cabbage (sliced)
⅓ cup carrots shredded
2 chopped green onions
⅓ cup finely chopped yellow onions
2 eggs
Sugar
White vinegar
2 cups vegetable oil
2 cloves garlic (peeled)

1. Choosing the right rice paper – It has been my experience to always try your best to select rice paper with "rice" listed as first ingredient. Rice paper with "tapioca" listed as first ingredient is tackier and harder to get crispy.

2. Place unseasoned ground chicken or ground pork in a large mixing bowl, add ¼ teaspoon salt, ½ teaspoon MSG, and ½ teaspoon paprika. (**Note:** Do not use any prepackaged ground pork that's seasoned.) Mix well and marinate for 15 minutes.

3. Add to bowl with marinated chicken or pork, ⅓ cup finely chopped yellow onions, 2 cups sliced green cabbage, ⅓ cup shredded carrots, 2 chopped green onions, 2 eggs, ¼ teaspoon salt, and ¾ teaspoon MSG. Mix until well blended and marinate for 15 minutes.

4. In large skillet, add 2 ½ cups water, 1 tablespoon sugar, and 2 tablespoons vinegar. Mix well and place over heat until water is hot but won't burn to touch. Remove from heat.

5. Take 1 sheet of rice paper and slip it under water in skillet until completely submerged. Remove immediately and shake off excess water before laying on cutting board or kitchen table.

6. Dab rice paper with paper towel to remove any remaining excess water.

7. Start out by soaking only 2-3 rice papers at a time. As you become more proficient in the process you will be able to prepare more egg rolls at one time.

8. Before moving on to the next step, allow a few seconds for the paper to soften enough to be pliable. Too much water will allow the paper to tear when rolling and break open while frying. Experience will teach you how moist to make the paper.

Continued next page →

Makes 12 large egg rolls

Egg Rolls (continued)

9. On all 3 prepared rice papers, add 2 tablespoons of chicken or pork mix 1½ inches up from lower edge. Leave at least 1 inch of space on each side of paper to allow for folding when rolling up.

10. Lift lower edge of paper and pull it up over chicken or pork mix. Begin rolling while keeping the rice paper tight to the pork mix. Roll paper almost half way up before folding the sides inward. Finish rolling while continuing to hold paper tight.

11. Place finished egg roll on plate or flat surface with ending edge of rice paper facing down. Repeat process until all of chicken or pork mix is used.

12. In large skillet, add 2 cups vegetable oil and 2 peeled garlic cloves, place over high heat. When you see garlic begin to fry, the oil is ready. Garlic adds a nice flavor to egg rolls but it's important to remove them before burning.

13. Add 6 egg rolls to skillet, allowing enough space between them for turning. Uncooked egg rolls will stick together if allowed to touch. If this happens, carefully use a spatula to assist in separating them. When using tongs or chopsticks for turning, always try grasping the portion of egg roll that's been exposed to the hot oil.

14. Cook over high heat for 6 minutes or until done, turning egg rolls every minute. Lower heat to medium. Remove egg rolls from skillet and place on bacon rack to allow to cool. If placed directly on a plate when hot, they will become mushy and sticky.

15. Cook remaining egg rolls over medium heat for 7 minutes or until done, turning every minute. (I recommend using medium heat with the second batch because vegetable oil is already hot and beginning to darken). Remove from skillet and place on bacon rack. Enjoy hot or cold!

Note: Left overs can be made crisp again in just a couple minutes by reheating in an oven or air fryer.

Use caution when deep frying egg rolls. Water trapped inside filling turns into steam and may cause hot oil to splatter.

Gourd or Chayote Soup

3 cups cooked rice
3 cups bottle gourd or chayote (sliced)
8 oz. chicken boneless skinless (sliced) or tender beef cut (sliced)
Salt, MSG, Black pepper
Olive oil
⅓ cup shallots or yellow onions (sliced)

2 cups chicken broth
⅓ cup sliced carrots
2-3 slices of ginger
Sugar
1-2 chopped green onions or cilantro

1. Cook white or brown rice and have ready.

2. If using bottle gourd, remove outer skin and slice. For chayote, remove outer skin and seed before slicing. Chayote is a little harder than gourds and will require additional cooking time if sliced the same thickness.

3. In a bowl, add 8 oz. chicken or tender beef cut, ¼ teaspoon salt, ½ teaspoon MSG, and a touch of black pepper. Mix well and set aside.

4. In medium size sauce pan, add 1½ tablespoons olive oil and ⅓ cup shallots or yellow onions. Place over medium heat and stir until onions turn golden brown. Add contents of bowl with chicken or beef.

5. Stir for 2 minutes then add 3 cups water and 1 cup chicken broth. Bring to a low boil and cook for 5 minutes if using chicken and 1 minute if using beef.

6. Add 3 cups sliced gourd or chayote, ⅓ cup sliced carrots, and 2-3 slices of ginger. Bring back to a low boil and cook for 5 minutes. Skim off any broth scum.

7. Add ¼ teaspoon salt, ¼ teaspoon MSG, and 1 teaspoon sugar. Cook for 1 minute and remove from heat.

8. Add a touch of black pepper, chopped green onions or cilantro, then allow to sit 5 minutes before serving with rice. Great with sweet and spicy fish sauce (page 55).

Note: I love to cook this dish because it's quick and delicious. I have it almost every night during the growing season. The best way to know a bottle gourd is ready is when it becomes slightly larger than the size of a rice bowl (4½" in diameter). During the winter months, I often buy chayote at the local market to replace the bottle gourd.

Serves 3

Green Papaya Salad
Gỏi đu đủ

Lime juice

Sugar

2 cloves chopped garlic

1 hot chili peppers (chopped)

Fish sauce

5-6 cups fresh green Papaya (shredded)

½ cup carrots (shredded)

1 cup yellow onions (thin sliced)

½ cup chopped cashews or your favorite nuts

1 hot chili pepper (thin sliced)

¼ cup fresh Vietnamese or Thai Basil (chopped)

1. In small bowl, add 1⅓ tablespoons lime juice, 2½ tablespoons sugar, 2 chopped garlic cloves, and 1 hot chili pepper. Lightly stir. Add 2½ tablespoons fish sauce, mix well then set aside.

2. In large bowl, add 5-6 cups shredded green papaya, ½ cup shredded carrots, and 1 cup thin sliced yellow onions. Mix well, add sauce bowl, then mix well again before serving on plate.

3. Top it off with chopped cashews or your favorite nuts, sliced hot chili pepper (optional), and chopped basil. This makes a great side dish and can be served as a main dish with sautéed shrimp (page 58).

Note: Leftovers will remain delicious for a couple of days when refrigerated.

Serves 4

Okra & Hamburger With Rice

- 3 cups cooked rice
- 10 oz. fresh ground beef (75/25)
- Salt, MSG, Black pepper
- 1 lb. fresh okra
- Olive oil
- ⅓ cup yellow onions (sliced)
- ½ cup carrots (sliced)
- Dark soy sauce
- ½ cup chicken stock
- 2 chopped green onions

1. Cook white or brown rice and have ready.

2. In mixing bowl, add 10 oz. ground beef, ¼ teaspoon salt, ¼ teaspoon MSG, and a pinch of black pepper. Mix well and allow to marinate while you prepare okra.

3. Wash and dry okra, then slice off the thicker end of pod which can be bitter and hard to chew. Cut okra into 1-1½ inch pieces and set aside.

4. In large skillet, add 1 teaspoon oil and ⅓ cup sliced yellow onion. Place over medium heat and stir until oil is hot. Add ground beef mix; stir and break up meat for 2½ minutes or until meat is mostly done, remove from heat.

5. Add cut okra, ½ cup sliced carrots, ½ teaspoon MSG, ¼ teaspoon salt, and 1 teaspoon dark soy sauce. Place over medium heat and stir for 2 minutes.

6. Add ½ cup chicken stock and ¾ cup water, stir and cover with lid. Cook for 6 minutes, remove lid and stir. Cook for an additional 5 minutes without cover while stirring often. Remove from heat, mix in chopped green onions, serve over rice and enjoy!

Note: Okra is great dipped in fish sauce or soy sauce mixed with your favorite hot pepper.

While I was growing up in Vietnam, nine out of ten people in my neighborhood grew okra. They planted it everywhere: all around their houses, in the garden, around ponds, and along the dirt paths leading to their homes.

Mom was always a great cook and could make many dishes using okra. One of my favorites was when she steamed them. While cooking rice, she'd lay fresh okra over it 15 minutes before the rice was done. When the rice was ready, she'd remove the okra with chopsticks leaving green indentations in the rice the shape of okra. That beautiful image remains in my head today.

DYNASTY
MAIFUN
RICE STICKS
NET WT. 6.75 OZ (191g)

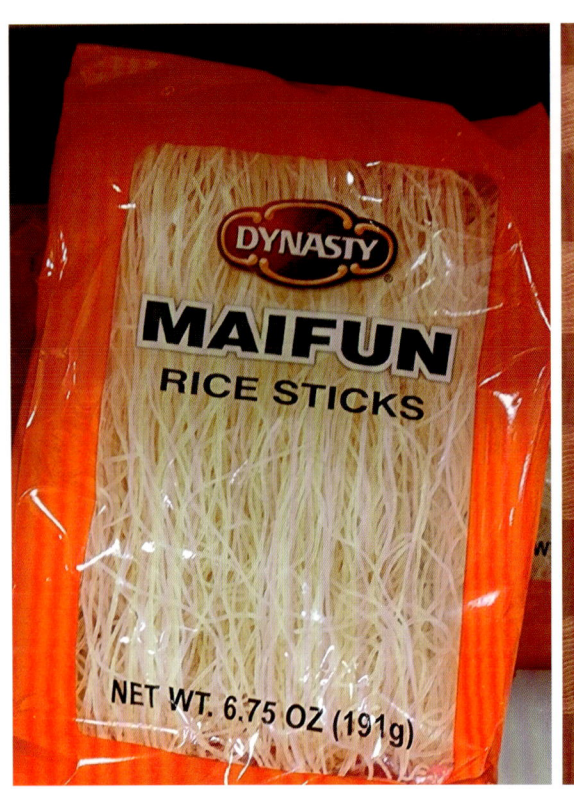

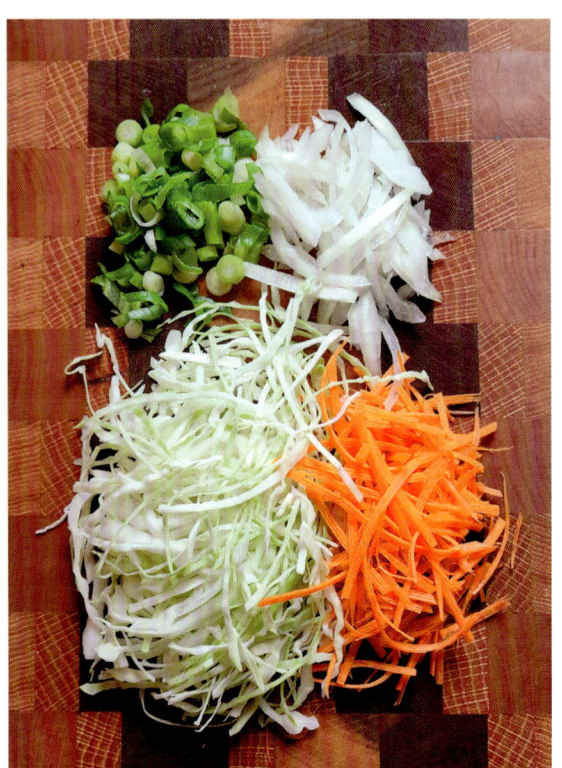

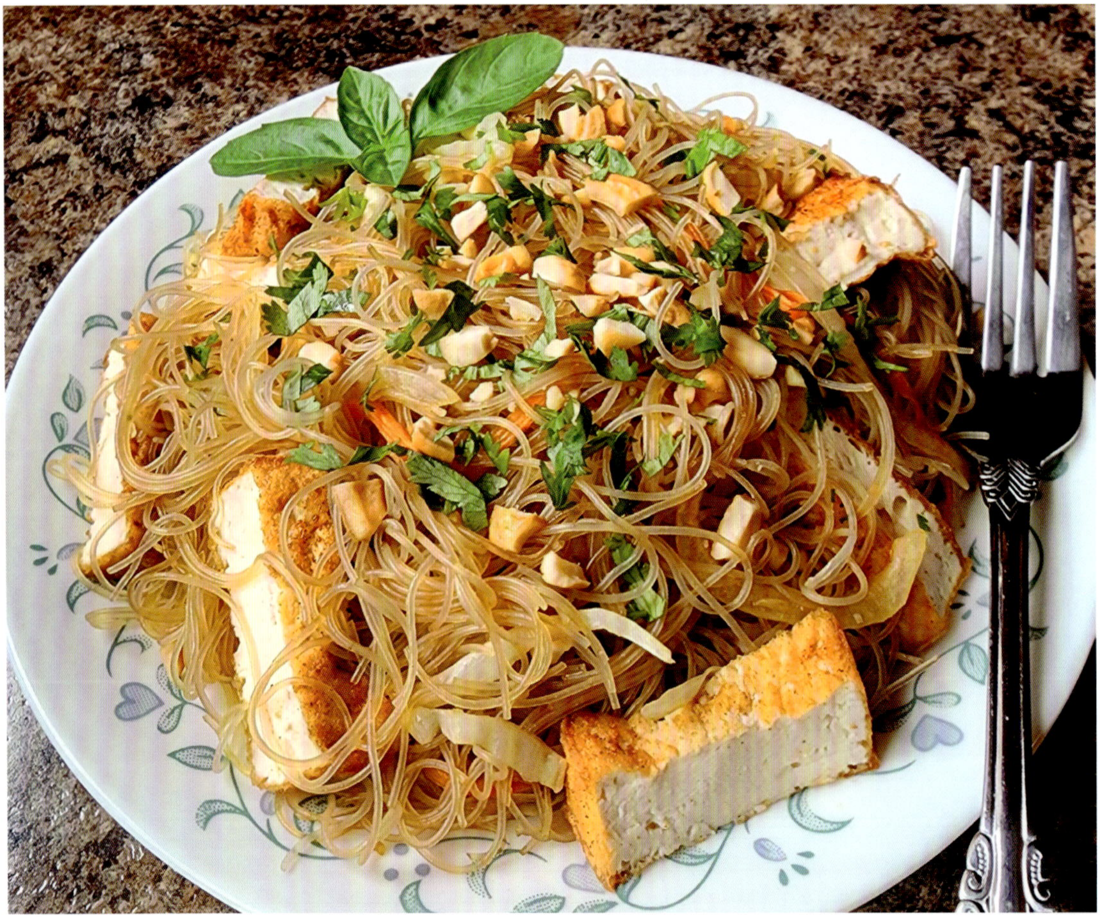

Rice Noodles With Cabbage

4 oz. dry rice noodles or rice sticks
1 cup green cabbage (sliced)
⅓ cup yellow onion (sliced)
MSG, Salt, Black pepper
Olive oil
2 cloves fresh garlic (chopped)
⅓ cup carrots (shredded)

1 green onion (chopped)
Soy sauce
1½ tablespoons chicken broth
Tofu (page 59) Shrimp (page 58)
Chopped cashews
Cilantro and basil (optional)

Note: There are two types of dry noodles you'll find in Asian markets. They're manufactured by many different companies and it's easy to be confused over which type to get. Both types are dry noodles and look very much alike. The ones labeled "Bun Tuoi" on the package are used in the recipe for Fresh Rice Noodle Bowl and for making spring rolls. After boiling they have a sticky texture and are heavy. The packaged noodles labeled with just the words "dried noodles" or "rice sticks" are excellent for frying and should be used in this dish. My preferred choice is Dynasty® brand "Maifun Rice Sticks", available at selected local grocery stores or online.

1. Begin by softening 4 oz. of Maifun Rice Sticks in hot tap water for 20 minutes. When noodles are soft, cut them in half with scissors while they're still in the water.

2. Transfer noodles into colander, allowing time for removal of any free water. In medium size bowl, add softened noodles, 1 cup sliced cabbage, ⅓ cup sliced yellow onion, ⅓ cup shredded carrots, 1 chopped green onion, ½ teaspoon MSG, ¼ teaspoon salt, and ⅛ teaspoon back pepper. Mix well.

3. In large skillet, add 1½ tablespoons olive oil and 2 cloves of fresh chopped garlic. Place over medium heat and stir well until garlic turns golden brown. Add contents of bowl with noodles and evenly spread out over skillet. Stir and turn for 2 minutes.

4. Remove from heat, add 1 tablespoon soy sauce and 1½ tablespoons chicken broth. Mix well. Place over medium heat, stir and mix for 3 minutes, cooking noodles to your personal liking. Adjust heat and add 2 tablespoons water if noodles are dry.

5. Remove from heat, mix in cilantro and basil (optional) and desired amount of tofu or shrimp. Empty skillet onto large plate and spread noodles out as soon as possible. This allows heat to escape, preventing noodles from breaking up by overcooking. Top with chopped cashews and serve alone or with Sweet and Spicy Fish Sauce (page 55). Enjoy!

Serves 2-3

PEARL RIVER BRIDGE
草菇老抽
MUSHROOM FLAVOURED
SUPERIOR DARK SOY SAUCE
天然釀造
Naturally Brewed
16.9 FL.OZ (500mL)

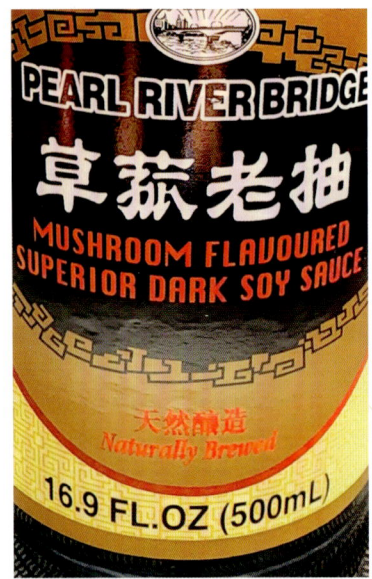

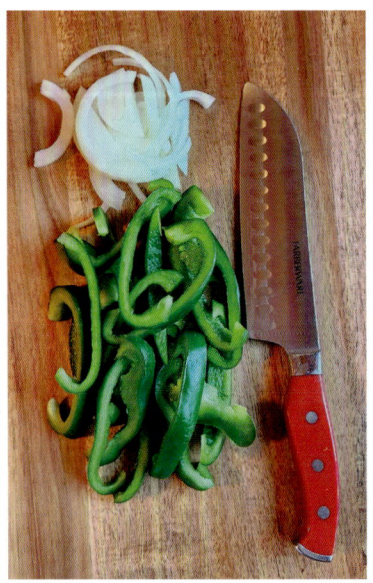

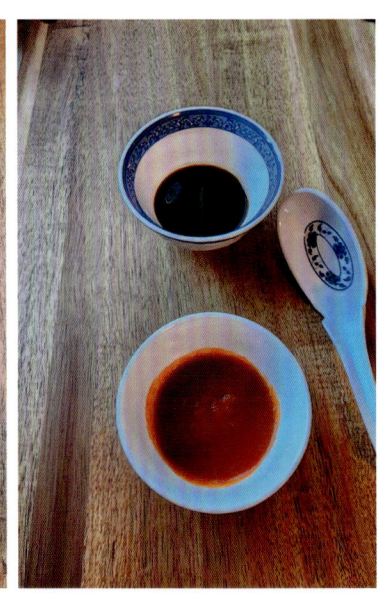

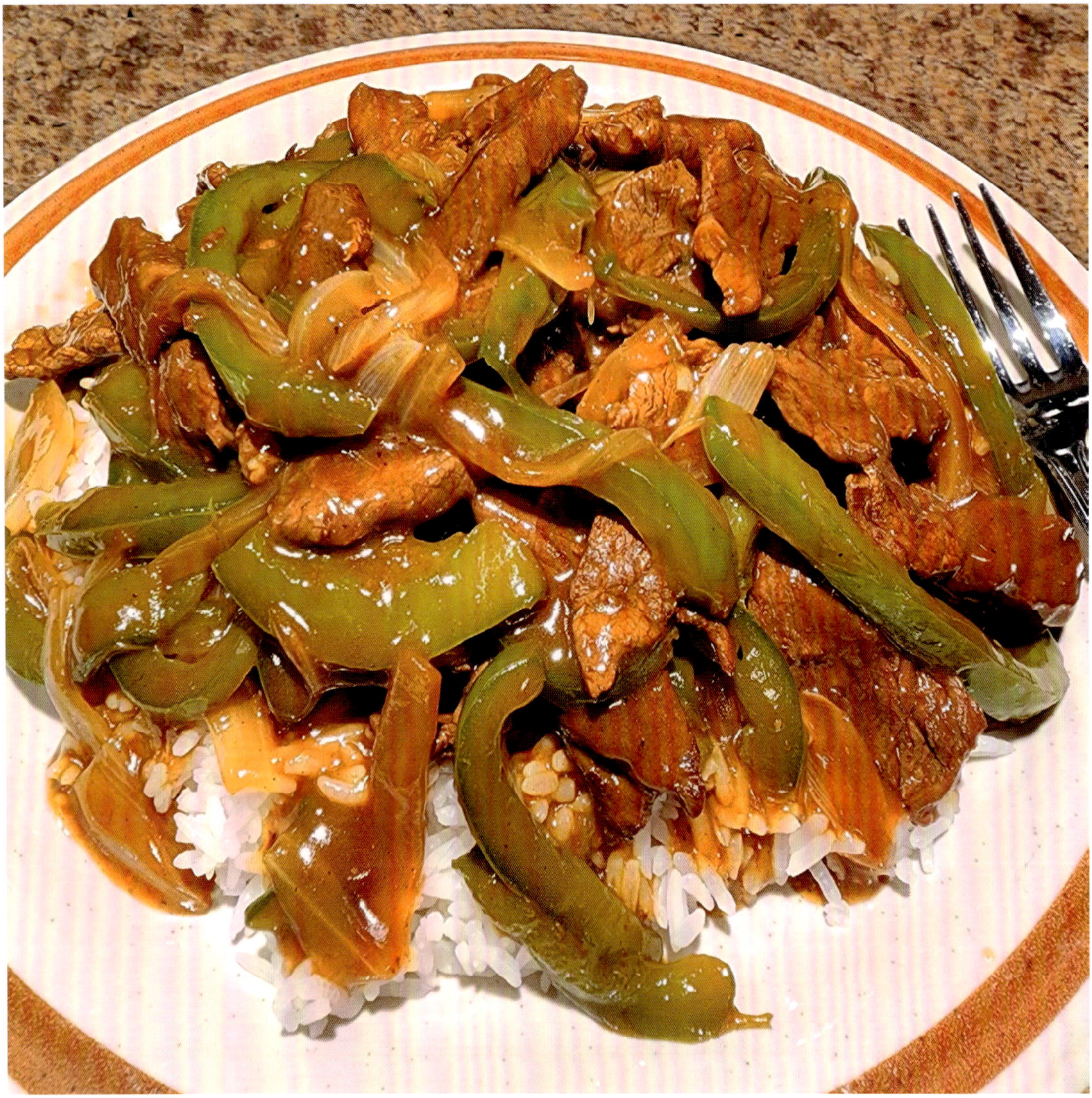

Pepper Steak Stir Fry With Rice

- 3 cups cooked rice
- 10 oz. tender beef cut (sliced)
- Salt
- MSG
- Garlic powder
- Black pepper
- Butter
- ½ cup sliced yellow onions
- 1 large green pepper (sliced)
- Dark soy sauce
- Sugar
- Corn starch

1. Cook white or brown rice and have ready

2. Cut 10 oz. tender beef cut into thin slices. To make slicing the steak easier, simply place your steak in the freezer beforehand until partially frozen.

3. In medium size bowl, add 10 oz. sliced tender beef cut, ½ teaspoon salt, ½ teaspoon MSG, ¼ teaspoon garlic powder, and a sprinkle of black pepper. Mix well.

4. In large skillet, add 2 tablespoons butter, place over high heat. As soon as butter melts, add ½ cup yellow onions and contents of prepared bowl of tender beef cut. Stir continuously for 1 minute or until meat is halfway cooked, remove from heat.

5. Add 2 cups green peppers, 1½ teaspoons dark soy sauce, ¼ teaspoon MSG, ½ teaspoon sugar, and 1/2 teaspoon salt.

6. Place over medium heat, stir for 2 minutes then add 2 cups water. Bring to a boil and cook for 3 minutes. Remove from heat.

7. In small sauce bowl, add 2 tablespoons corn starch with ¼ cup cool water. Mix well. Over medium heat, slowly pour mixture into stir fry and continuously stir for 1-3 minutes, depending on how well done you like your green peppers.

8. If you prefer a thicker gravy add more corn starch, or just add water to make it thinner. Remove from heat and serve over rice. Enjoy!

Note: When I owned my restaurant, I served this dish with an egg roll along with soy sauce and/or sriracha hot chili sauce.

Serves 3

Pork & Fish Sauce With Rice

- 1 lb. pork belly or pork shoulder
- Salt, Garlic powder, MSG, Sugar
- 3 cups cooked rice
- Extra virgin olive oil
- 1/3 cup chopped yellow onion
- 1 teaspoon dark soy sauce
- 3 tablespoons fish sauce
- 1 fresh hot chili pepper
- 3 boiled and peeled eggs
- 1 chopped green onion

1. In medium size bowl, add 1lb pork (cleaned and cut into large bite-size pieces), ½ teaspoon salt, ½ teaspoon garlic powder, ½ teaspoon MSG, and 1 tablespoon sugar. Mix well and allow to sit for 30-45 minutes.

2. Cook rice and have ready. Boil eggs and peel.

3. In medium size saucepan, add 1 tablespoon olive oil, ⅓ cup chopped yellow onion. Place over high heat and stir until oil is hot.

4. Add prepared bowl with pork and stir for 2 minutes or until the pork and onions begin to brown. Add 1 teaspoon dark soy sauce, stir constantly for a minute or two to avoid burning and ensuring pork is coated with soy sauce.

5. Add 3 cups of water, 3 tablespoons fish Sauce, 1 tablespoon sugar, 1 chopped hot chili pepper, and 3 boiled eggs (peeled). Allow to cook over medium-low heat for 30 minutes. Remove from heat, mix in chopped green onion, serve and enjoy!

Note: Serve with rice, cucumbers, or any of your favorite vegetables. Also great when served with "Sweet Rice and Mung Beans" (page 67).

When I was young, we could only afford ¼ pound of pork every so often. Mom used that pork to make this dish and we all felt like we were in heaven. To make sure there was enough to go around for all six of us, Mom would make it very salty, so salty that if you were not careful, your tongue would curl up.

Years later, when we had a little more money, she'd buy a larger amount of pork for celebrating the Vietnamese New Year and even added some boiled eggs to it (with a lot less salt).

My daughter, Melissa, lives in New York City and loves to cook for her friends. One day she called to ask how to make this dish. She had a group of friends coming over that night and wanted to prepare it for them. I tried talking her out of it because it's been my experience that people in America find the smell of cooking with fish sauce offensive. Her immediate reply was, "It'll be fine, I'll just open a window!

Serves 3

Bitter Melon Soup With Meat Balls

⅓ cup bean thread vermicelli noodles
⅓ cup dried black fungus
   (Shredded woodear mushroom)
12 oz. ground pork without seasoning
Salt
MSG
Black pepper
2 eggs

3 medium size bitter melon
2 cups chicken broth
Sugar
Fish sauce
1-2 chopped green onions
1 chopped chili pepper (optional)
4 cups cooked rice

1. Soak ½ oz. or ⅓ cup bean thread vermicelli noodles in warm water for 8 minutes, rinse and drain off water, making sure no excess water remains. Finely chop noodles and set aside. Note: To aid in measuring noodles, soak 1 complete section from package, finely chop, measure, and discard remaining chopped noodles.

2. Soak ⅓ cup shredded black fungus for 8 minutes in warm water. Rinse 3 times while squeezing fungus with your hands to aid in cleaning. Drain off water, making sure no excess water remains. Finely chop and set aside.

3. Wash and cut bitter melon in half lengthwise, then use small spoon to scoop out seeds. Cut melon into 2-inch-long pieces, set aside.

4. In bowl, add 12 oz. ground pork without seasoning, ½ teaspoon salt, ½ teaspoon MSG, a touch of black pepper, chopped vermicelli noodles, chopped black fungus, and 2 eggs. Mix and stir for 5 minutes or until the right consistency is reached, set aside.

5. In 4 quart sauce pan, add 6 cups water, 2 cups chicken broth, and ½ tablespoon sugar. Place over high heat and bring to boil. Begin rolling pork mixture into small meat balls, gently adding them to boiling sauce pan one at a time. Do not stir.

6. Bring back to a boil and cook over medium heat for 5 minutes.

7. Add bitter melon, bring back to a boil and cook over medium heat for 10 minutes while stirring occasionally.

Continued next page →

Serves 4

Bitter Melon Soup With Meat Balls (continued)

8. Add ½ tablespoon fish sauce, ½ teaspoon salt, and ½ teaspoon MSG. Cook for an additional 15 minutes while continuing to stir occasionally.

9. Remove from heat, add chopped green onions, 1 chopped chili pepper (optional) and serve with rice. Enjoy!

Notes:

- Bitter melon, a member of the gourd family, is reported to have several great health benefits. Dipping it in fish sauce with hot chili peppers gives it a nice flavor while offsetting its inherent slight bitterness.

There are various types of bitter melons available for purchase, but the ones most found in Asian markets, characterized by a smooth surface between the grooves, are my preferred choice. Compared to the lumpy, darker-skinned varieties, these smoother ones tend to be less bitter.

In Vietnam, it's common to stuff the meat mixture inside the whole bitter melon after removing its seeds through a single cut along its length. However, considering the labor-intensive nature of this process, I've found that creating meatballs and cutting the melon into pieces gives an equally delicious result!

- Bean thread noodles and woodear mushrooms are used only in this recipe. To avoid having unusable ingredients lying around your kitchen, I recommend you first prepare "Bitter Melon With Egg" (page 9) before making this dish. Bitter melon's unique flavor is an acquired taste worth taking your time to experiment with.

BÚN TƯƠI
TUFOCO
BAMBOO TREE
SẢN XUẤT TẠI MỸ THO - VIỆT NAM
FRESH RICE VERMICELLI
PRODUCT OF VIETNAM

BÁNH TRÁNG
EXTRA THIN
RICE PAPER
DOUBLE PARROT
HƯƠNG VỊ QUÊ NHÀ
CÔ GÁI VIỆT NAM
ĐẶC BIỆT MỎNG & DẺO
INGREDIENTS: RICE FLOUR, TAPIOCA FLOUR, SALT, WATER.
SPRING ROLL WRAPPER
NET WT : 20 OZ (570G)
Distributor : IHA BEVERAGE
COMMERCE, CA 90040
PRODUCT OF VIETNAM

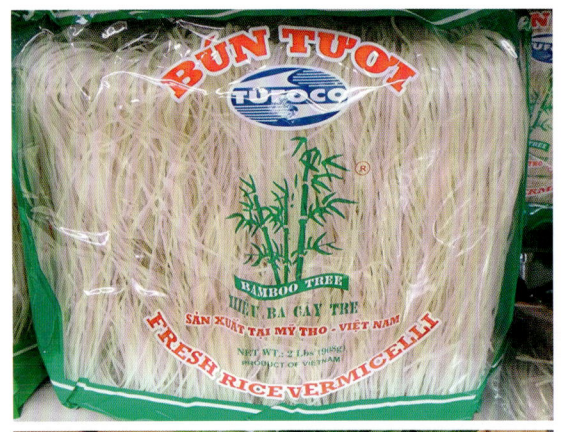

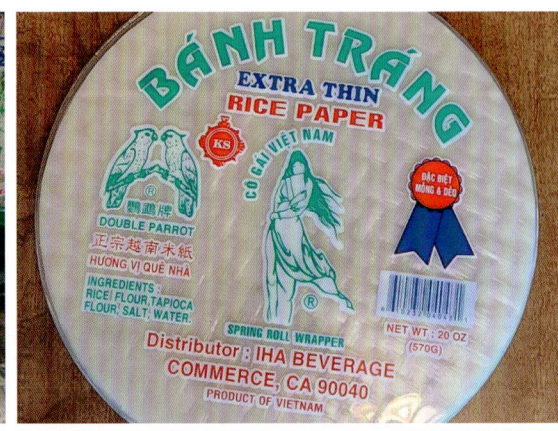

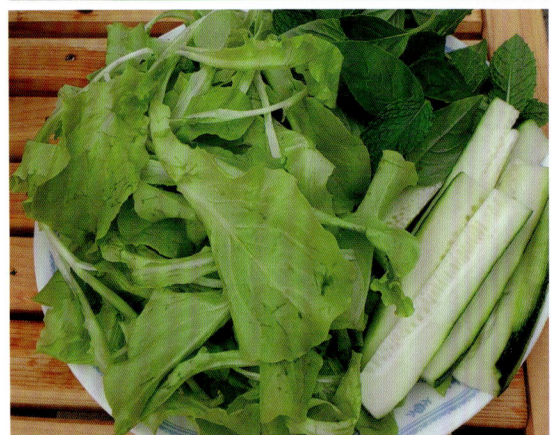

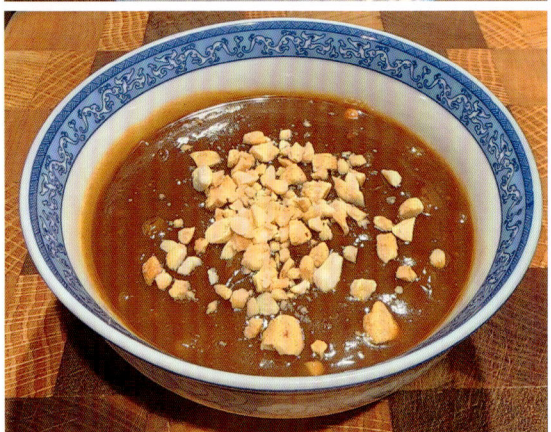

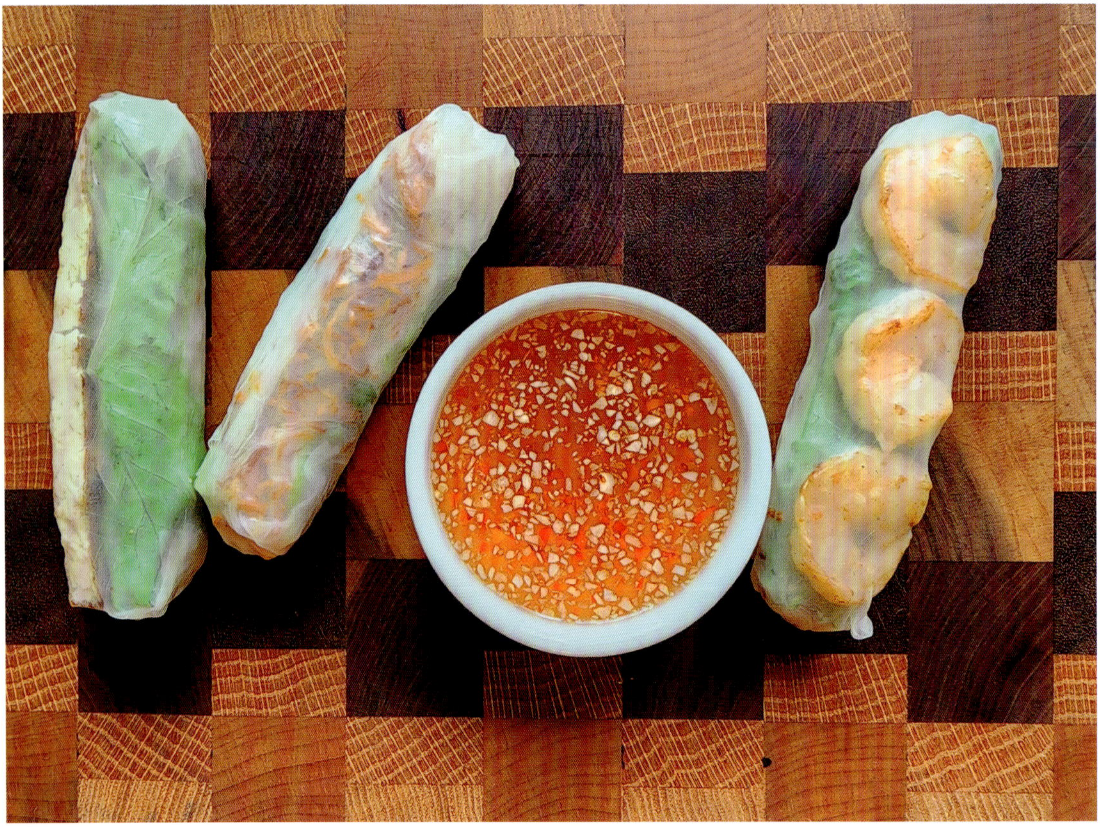

Fresh Spring Rolls

8 oz. Vietnamese rice vermicelli (bun tuoi)

1 Pack - Rice Paper

Green leaf lettuce

Crispy sweet potatoes*

Fresh mint leaves

Cucumbers

*Added ingredients and dips

Page #

Crispy sweet potatoes 57

Sautéed shrimp 58

Pork belly or shoulder 61

Crispy Tofu 59

Sweet and Spicy Fish Sauce . . . 55

Peanut Butter and Hoisin 56

There are two types of dry noodles you'll find in Asian markets. They're manufactured by many different companies and it's easy to be confused over which type to get. Both types are dry noodles and look very much alike. The ones labeled "Bun Tuoi" on the package are used for making spring rolls and for fresh rice noodle bowls. After boiling they hold together and are softer.

1. Prepare choice of sauce and meat.

2. Boil noodles (follow package instructions), set aside.

3. Make sure vegetables are clean and free of water.

4. Dip rice paper, one at a time, in a pan of warm water for one second to soften and shake off excess water. I sometimes just quickly hold under warm running tap water.

5. Lay softened rice paper on a wetted cutting board and place a piece of lettuce on lower portion of paper starting 1½ inches up from lower edge.

6. Add noodles, crispy sweet potatoes, vegetables, and meat of your choice*. Leave at least 1" space on each side of rice paper to allow for folding when rolling up. Word of caution, adding too much filling will make it difficult to roll up.

7. Lift the lower edge of rice paper and pull it up over filling. Begin rolling forward while holding the filling together and keeping the rice paper tight. Roll paper ½ of the way up before folding the sides inward. Finish rolling while continuing to hold paper tight.

Note: Serve with Sweet and Spicy Fish Sauce or Peanut Butter and Hoisin sauce.*

Makes 12 rolls

Steak & Mustard Greens

8-12 oz. ribeye steak
Salt
Black pepper
MSG
10 oz. mustard or turnip greens

Butter
3 cloves garlic (chopped)
½ cup carrots (Cut into thin strips)
Chicken Broth
2 cups cooked rice

1. Cook white or brown rice and have ready.

2. Place 8-12 oz. steak on plate (ribeye or your favorite choice), season with ¼ teaspoon salt, black pepper, and ¼ teaspoon MSG. Allow to marinate for 15-30 minutes.

3. Lay 10 oz. mustard or turnip greens on cutting board and remove hard section from bottom of stems. Remove any bad leaves then cut greens into 2 or 3 pieces. Wash greens thoroughly and drain off excess water.

4. In small skillet, cook steak to your personal liking and set aside. Save any grease in skillet to add into greens later (optional).

5. In large skillet, add 1 tablespoon butter and 3 chopped garlic cloves. Place over high heat and stir until garlic browns, remove from heat. Add carrots, mustard greens, ¼ teaspoon of salt, ¼ teaspoon MSG, and a sprinkle of black pepper. Place back over high heat, stir for 1-2 minutes, remove from heat.

6. Add any leftover grease from small skillet and 2 tablespoons chicken broth. Place back over high heat, stir for 2-4 more minutes, depending on how well done you prefer your vegetables. Remove from heat and transfer vegetables to plate.

7. Slice steak into thin or medium size pieces and add to vegetable plate.

8. Serve with rice, Sweet and Spicy Fish Sauce (page 55), or soy sauce and hot peppers. Enjoy!

Serves 2

Fried Fish With Vietnamese Sauce

3 cups cooked rice
Fresh lime juice
Sugar
2 cloves garlic (chopped)
1 hot chili pepper (chopped)
Fish sauce
12 oz. Walleye fillet
All purpose flower
Corn starch
MSG, Salt
Vegetable oil
2 garlic cloves (peeled)
Ginger (thin strips)
1 tablespoon shallots or yellow onion (chopped)
⅓ cup cucumber (sliced)
1 tbsp. lime (cut up without skin)
1 tbsp. cilantro (chopped)
⅓ cup cashews

1. Cook white or brown rice and have ready.

2. In medium size bowl, add 1 teaspoon lime juice, 2 tablespoons sugar, 2 chopped garlic cloves, 1 chopped hot chili pepper, 1½ tablespoons fish sauce, and 4 tablespoons water. Mix well and set aside.

3. Make sure fish is thawed and cleaned. Used paper towels to remove any excess water if necessary. Make 2 or 3 cuts across each fillet to aid in cooking time.

4. In medium size bowl, add 3 tablespoons flower and 3 tablespoons corn starch, ½ teaspoon MSG, and ¼ teaspoon salt. Mix well and dip each fish fillet in mixture, coating both sides of fillet. Shake off any loose powder before placing on plate.

5. In a medium skillet, add 1 cup vegetable oil, 2 garlic cloves. Place over high heat until the garlic bubbles then add fish fillets. Garlic adds a nice flavor but must be removed before burning. Fry fillets for 2-4 minutes on each side until golden brown or cooked to your liking. Remove from heat, transfer fish to plate and allow to rest for 5 minutes.

6. Top fillets with ½ tablespoon fresh ginger cut into small strips, 1 tablespoon chopped shallots or yellow onion, ⅓ cup sliced cucumber, 1 tablespoon chopped lime, and ⅓ cup cashews. Finish topping everything off with contents of sauce bowl and 1 tablespoon chopped cilantro. This dish is best served with rice. Enjoy!

Serves 3

Rice Soup With Chicken & Mushrooms

- 8 oz. Boneless skinless chicken
- Salt, MSG, Black pepper
- 8 oz. oyster mushrooms
- Olive oil
- 2 garlic cloves (finely chopped)
- ¾ cup uncooked jasmine rice
- 3 cups chicken broth
- ⅓ cup chopped carrots
- 2-3 slices of ginger
- 2 chopped green onions

1. In bowl, add chicken that's been cleaned and cut into thin slices or cubes, ¼ teaspoon salt, ¼ teaspoon MSG, and sprinkle of black pepper. Mix well then allow to sit for 30 minutes.

2. In large bowl, soak mushrooms in lukewarm water with 1 teaspoon salt for 5 minutes. Using your hands, gently stir mushrooms around then drain water. Refill bowl with fresh water and again gently stir before draining. Repeat filling bowl and stirring 2 more times, then cut larger mushrooms into 2-4 pieces. Set aside.

3. In skillet, add 1 tablespoon olive oil and 2 finely chopped garlic cloves. Place over high heat. When garlic begins to brown, add seasoned chicken and stir for 3 minutes. Remove from heat, set aside.

4. In 4 quart sauce pan, add ¾ cup rinsed jasmine rice, 3 cups chicken broth, and 3 cups water. Bring to a boil.

5. Add chicken from skillet, cook with a low boil for 15 minutes while occasionally stirring.

6. Add 3 cups water and bring back to a low boil. Add 8 oz. mushrooms, ⅓ cup chopped carrots, 2-3 slices of ginger, and ½ teaspoon MSG. Continue cooking for 20 minutes while stirring more often. Remove from heat, mix in chopped green onions and enjoy!

Serves 4-6

Meatloaf

2 cups milk
¾ cup chopped yellow onions
6 eggs
Salt, MSG, Paprika
Garlic powder

Sugar, Ketchup, Black pepper
Tumeric (optional)
1½ cups oatmeal (quick oats)
6 slices white bread
3 lbs. ground beef (75/25)

1. In large bowl, add 2 cups milk, ¾ cup chopped yellow onions, 6 eggs, 2½ teaspoons salt, 2 teaspoons MSG, 1 teaspoon paprika, 1 teaspoon garlic powder, 2 teaspoons sugar, 1 tablespoon ketchup, ¼ teaspoon of black pepper, and ½ teaspoon tumeric (optional). Mix well then add, 1 cup oatmeal, 6 slices white bread (toasted crispy and crumbled into small pieces), and 3 lbs. ground beef. Stir and mix until well blended, allow to sit for 30 minutes.

2. In bowl, add ¾ cup ketchup and 2 tablespoons sugar. Mix well and set aside.

3. Spread a thin layer of butter in bottom and sides of a 9" x 13" baking pan, then add ground beef mix into pan. Using your hands, crown ground beef mix to pan's center, allowing grease to run over to and down both sides of pan when baking.

4. Pre-heat oven to 350°, cover pan with foil and place on next to bottom rack. Bake for 60 minutes.

5. Remove foil, completely cut meatloaf lengthwise and widthwise across center of pan to allow heat penetration. Recover with foil and continue baking for 20 minutes.

6. Uncover and carefully remove ½ of grease in pan. Spread ketchup and sugar mix on top of meatloaf, then bake for an additional 10 minutes without cover.

7. Remove from heat and allow to rest for 10 minutes before serving.

Note: I prefer using 75/25 ground beef because it gives the meatloaf a softer texture. This dish is usually served with mashed potatoes, but my family enjoys it with rice, cut up fresh vegetables, and fish sauce. Whenever I don't have time to prepare more than one dish, I always make this awesome meatloaf. Everyone loves it!

Serves 10-12

Inn Maid
KLUSKI
EGG NOODLES
NET WT. 8 OZ (227g)

Mrs. Miller's
Gluten Free
SOUP BASE
Chicken Flavored
Soup Base

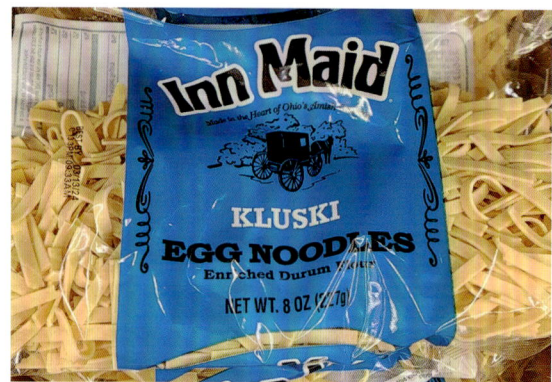

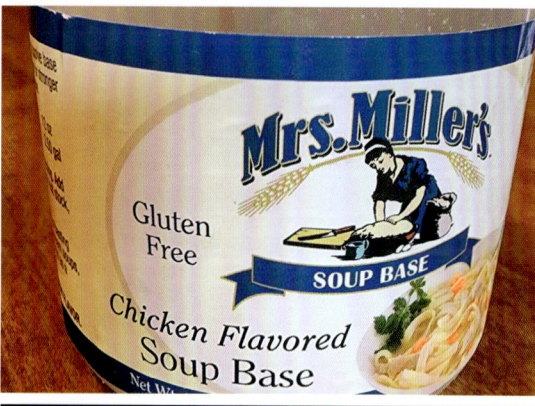

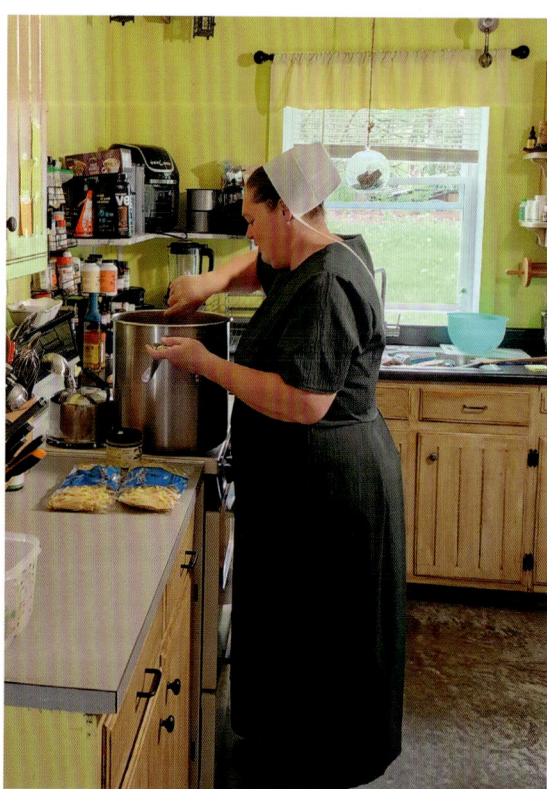

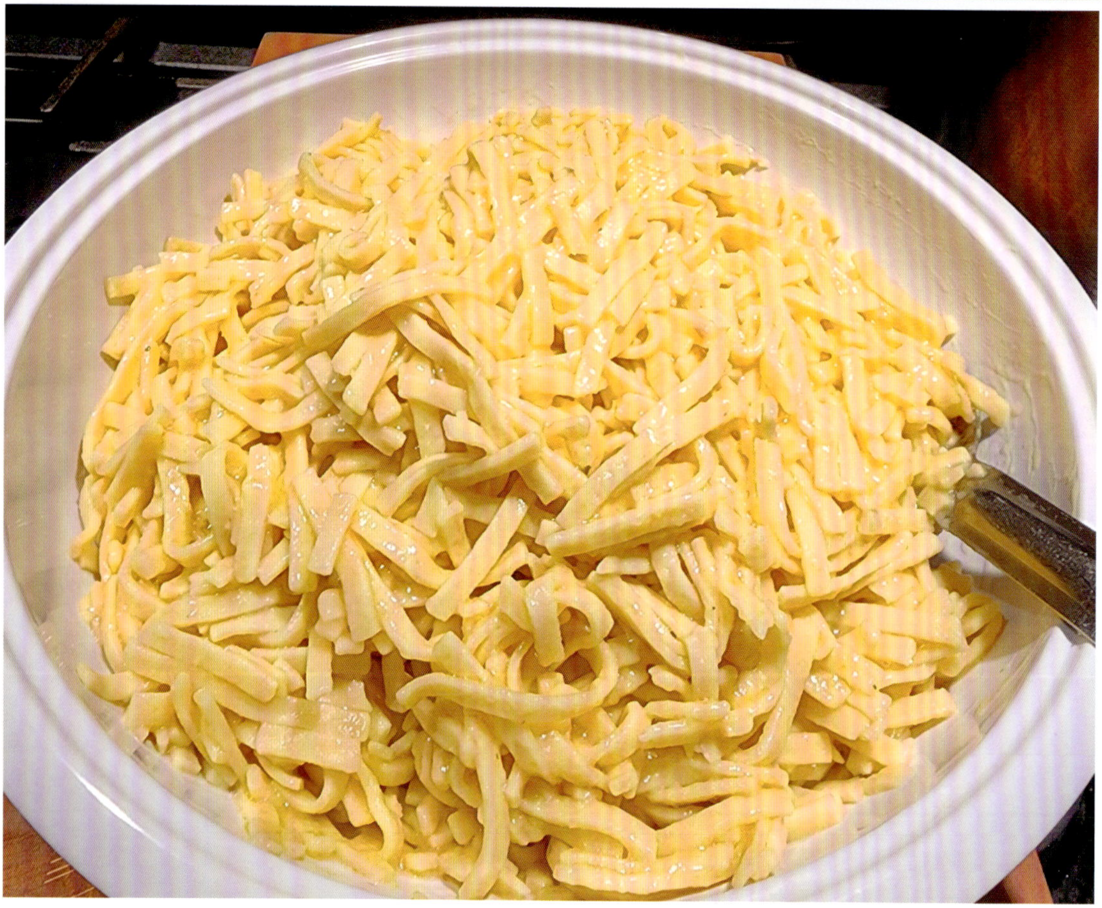

Amish Noodles

1 stick butter (8 tbsp)

2 - 10 oz. cans Cream of chicken soup

Chicken base

2½ cups chicken stock

3 cups water

16 oz. noodles (Inn-Maid ®)

1. In 4 quart sauce pan, add 1 stick butter and place over medium-low heat. When butter is melted, add 2 - 10 oz. cans cream of chicken soup. When hot, add 1 tablespoon chicken base. Stir until well blended.

2. Add 2½ cups chicken stock, 3 cups water and stir well. Cover and bring to a boil, stirring occasionally because it will stick to the bottom!!

3. When boiling, add noodles a little at a time or it will boil over. Stir and bring back to a boil. Cook for 1 minute, remove from heat and cover. Do not stir and do not add salt. Allow to stand for at least 1 hour before serving. Mix in more water if necessary.

Note: I love this noodle dish! I got it from a good Amish friend who was kind enough to share her family recipe. It's very simple to make, but yet so good. The first time I prepared this dish was for Easter dinner and everyone loved it. They even took leftovers home with them.

The original recipe given to me was made with the intentions of serving 35 people. I've taken the liberty of reducing the ingredients for serving smaller groups.

Serves 14

Lasagna

- 1 lb. ground beef (75/25)
- MSG
- Salt
- Black pepper
- Olive oil
- 1/3 cup yellow onion (finely chopped)
- 2-24 oz. jars spaghetti sauce
- 1 package lasagna noodles
- 16 oz. cottage cheese
- 12 oz. shredded cheddar cheese

1. In bowl, add 1 lb. ground beef, ¼ teaspoon MSG, ¼ teaspoon salt, and a touch of black pepper. Mix well and set aside for 20-30 minutes.

2. In skillet, add 1 tablespoon olive oil and ⅓ cup yellow onion. Place over medium heat, stir until onions begin to brown, then add seasoned ground beef. Completely break up ground beef with spatula and cook for 3-5 minutes or until done. Set aside.

3. Spread 1 cup of spaghetti sauce in bottom of a 9"x 13"x 2" baking pan. Cover pasta sauce with a layer of uncooked lasagna noodles, breaking noodles if needed to cover entire pan bottom.

4. Spread 1 cup layer of spaghetti sauce over noodles, then sprinkle ⅓ of cooked ground beef over spaghetti sauce. Using a small spoon, dab ⅓ of cottage cheese randomly placed over ground beef layer. Sprinkle 3 oz. shredded cheese over cottage cheese layer, then add a layer of lasagna noodles. Repeat this layering process two more times leaving out the final layer of lasagna noodles. Top everything off with a 1½ cup layer of spaghetti sauce, a 3 oz. layer of shredded cheese, and a final ½ cup of spaghetti sauce lightly scattered over the top.

5. Do not preheat the oven. Cover pan with foil and place on center rack. Set oven temperature at 325°, bake for 60 minutes then remove foil cover. Increase oven temperature to 350°, bake for 10 more minutes then remove from oven. Allow to cool for 20-30 minutes before serving.

Note: I make this dish often because everyone loves it at my house. Leftovers is just as good as fresh baked. The extra sauce and cottage cheese allows it to remain soft and juicy.

Serves 6-8

Sweet and Spicy Fish Sauce

2 cloves garlic
3 chili peppers (adjust to taste)
1 tablespoon lime juice

⅓ cup sugar
¾ cup water
¼ cup fish sauce

1. Chop garlic and chili peppers into fine pieces, place in soup bowl
2. Add 1 tablespoon lime juice, ⅓ cup sugar, ¾ cup water, and ¼ cup fish sauce
3. Mix well, adjust ingredients to taste

Note: Refrigerated sauce mix will keep for a couple of days. Frozen chili peppers can be used same as fresh for a few months.

Sweet and Spicy Fish Sauce With Carrots
Great with fried rice recipes

1. In small bowl, add ⅓ cup shredded carrots, ¼ cup Sweet and Spicy Fish Sauce
2. Allow to sit 15 minutes
3. Add 1 tablespoon chopped cashews

Peanut Butter & Hoisin Sauce

Vegetarian Hoisin Sauce

Creamy peanut butter

Water

Chopped nuts (Peanut or Cashew)

1. In small bowl, add 2 tablespoons hoisin sauce and 2 tablespoons creamy peanut butter, stir with fork until well blended. Slowly add 4 tablespoons water while continuing to stir until reaching consistency of your liking. Add nuts, serve and enjoy!

2. This sauce and the Sweet and Spicy Fish Sauce are both excellent for using with spring rolls.

Note: Vegetarian and regular Hoisin Sauce have distinctively different tastes and we strongly recommend using the vegetarian type with this recipe.

Crispy Shredded Sweet Potato

1 large sweet potato   Vegetable oil   Salt (optional)

1. Peel, wash, and dry sweet potato then shred using a Julienne peeler. Slices 2 inches or longer is best.

2. Add 1¼ cups vegetable oil into 10-inch skillet, place over medium heat. Place 1 piece of sweet potato in oil to know when oil is ready, then remove. Add 1 cup shredded potatoes and fry for 2½ minutes then remove from heat.

3. Potatoes can burn quickly, so closely watch as they continue to fry. Place back over medium heat if necessary then immediately remove from heat again when potatoes begin turning golden brown.

4. Experience will be your best teacher in knowing when to remove potatoes from skillet. Remaining batches will require only 1½ minutes frying before first removing from heat.

3. Place on paper towels to remove excess oil and add a touch of salt (optional). Repeat process until all potatoes are fried.

Note: Shredded sweet potatoes are very bitter when burnt. If you accidentally burn them, throw out that batch or you'll destroy the flavor of your dish. Shredded sweet potatoes are delicious in spring rolls, rice noodle bowls, and also make a great snack.

Sautéed Shrimp

For use in Spring Roll or Papaya Salad

12 oz. large shrimp	Paprika	½ cup sliced shallot or yellow onions
Salt,	Olive oil	
MSG	2 chopped garlic cloves	Butter

1. In a bowl, add 12 oz. large shrimp (make sure shrimp is peeled, thawed, clean, and free of water), ¼ teaspoon salt, ¼ teaspoon MSG, and ¼ teaspoon paprika. Toss well and set aside.

2. In skillet, add 1 tablespoon olive oil, 2 chopped garlic cloves, and ½ cup chopped shallot or yellow onion. Place over high heat and stir until onions and garlic begin to brown. Add shrimp bowl then stir and turn for 1 minute. Add 1 tablespoon butter and continue to stir and turn for 3-4 minutes or until cooked to your liking.

3. Remove from heat and add to Fresh Spring Rolls, Green Papaya Salad, or your favorite dish.

nasoya
ORGANIC TOFU
FIRM
AMERICA'S #1 SELLING TOFU BRAND
NET WT. 14 OZ (397 g)
House Foods
tofu
PREMIUM
Delicious in soups and lasagnas!
MEDIUM FIRM
How Firm is Medium Firm?
1 2 3 4 5 6
PERISHABLE • KEEP REFRIGERATED
STORE IN WATER
NET WT. 19 OZ (1 LB 3 OZ) 538 g

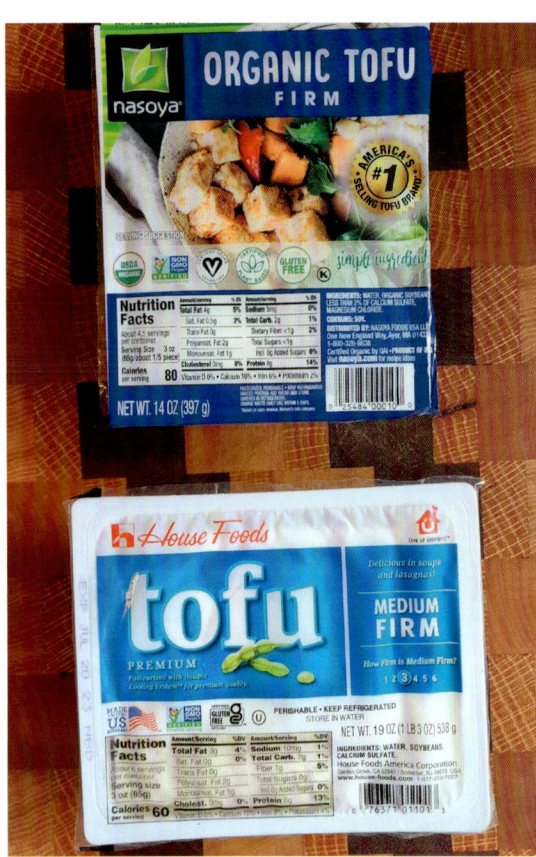

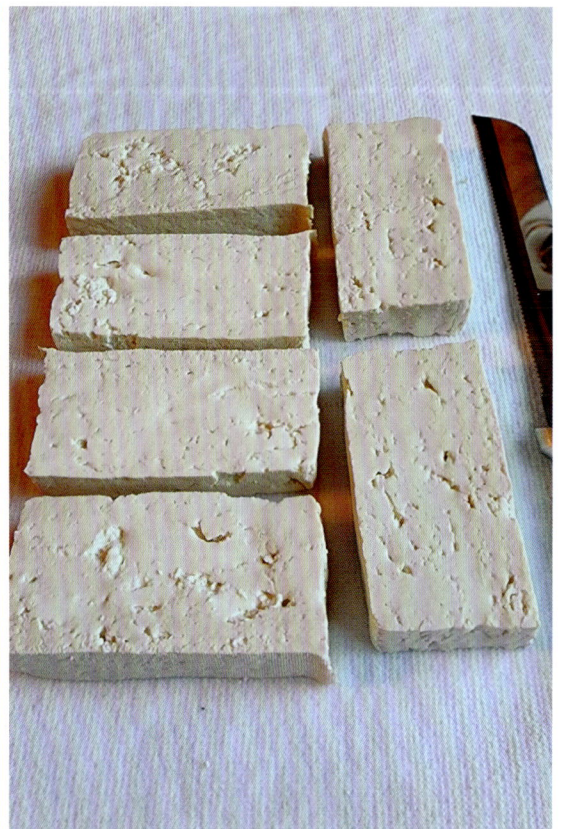

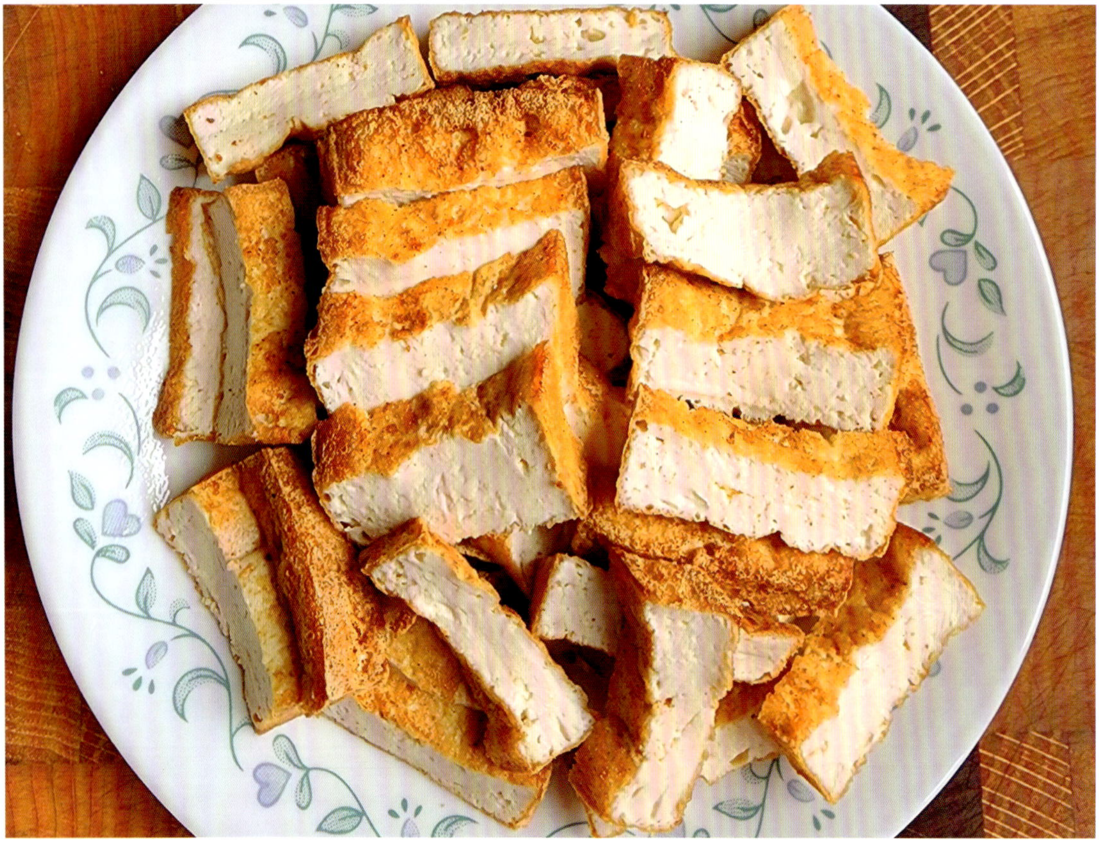

Crispy Tofu

1 package of Tofu
Olive oil
Paprika

MSG, Salt
½ cup vegetable oil
1 clove garlic (peeled & halved)

Note: For use in spring rolls and rice noodles. Also delicious served with rice and vegetables.

1. Drain tofu and carefully lay out on cutting board. Cut into 6 equal slices, the short way. Arrange the slices on cotton towel, then pat the top of tofu with paper towels using light pressure. It's important to remove any excess water. Allow tofu to rest for 15 minutes.

2. In a small sauce bowl, add 1 tablespoon olive oil, ½ teaspoon paprika, ⅛ teaspoon MSG, and ⅛ teaspoon salt; mix well.

3. Carefully remove tofu from towel, brush olive oil mixture on both sides and edges, place on plate. Use care to not break the tofu. Allow to marinate for 15 minutes.

4. In 10 inch skillet, add ½ cup vegetable oil and 1 clove garlic peeled and halved. Place over medium heat, adding tofu as soon as oil is hot. Cook for 5 minutes then carefully turn over and remove garlic. Cook for an additional 5-7 minutes or until your liking. Remove from heat and transfer tofu to bacon rack.

Note: As a child in Vietnam, I always loved watching a lady at the market fry and sell tofu for a living. She always had the biggest smile while sitting on the ground conducting business. Her expertly maintained fire built under a Vietnamese wood stove supplied the proper heat to a large frying pan sitting on top. The lady used very long chopsticks, frying hundreds of tofu every day.

It was fascinating to see her work. I always wondered how she could fry tofu, make sales, and keep a perfect fire going at the same time, all without burning any.

Boiled & Sliced Pork

For use in Banh Xeo and Spring Rolls

1 lb. pork belly or pork shoulder blade
Salt & MSG

1. Cut pork belly or pork shoulder blade into 2 or 3 pieces to aid in cooking.

2. In medium size sauce pan, add 5 cups water, ½ teaspoon of salt, and ½ teaspoon MSG.

3. Bring to a boil and add pork. Cook over medium heat for 30 minutes if using pork shoulder blade, and 45 minutes if using pork belly. Boil longer if necessary making sure pork is thoroughly cooked. Add more water if needed due to evaporation. Allow to cool before slicing in thin strips.

Sweet & Sour Kohlrabi & Carrots

Salt

⅓ cup sugar

½ cup vinegar

2 heaping cups kohlrabi (shredded)

1 heaping cup carrots (shredded)

2 cloves garlic (chopped)

1 hot chili pepper (chopped)

1. In medium size sauce pan, add 2 cups water, ¼ teaspoon salt, ⅓ cup sugar, and ½ cup vinegar. Give contents a quick stir before placing over heat. Continue stirring until sugar is completely dissolved and water comes to a boil.

2. Remove from heat and allow to sit until contents are room temperature.

3. Mix 2 heaping cups shredded kohlrabi and 1 heaping cup shredded carrots together then spread out on a double layer of paper towels. Allow to sit 10 minutes then add to quart jar.

4. Making sure sugar, vinegar, and water mixture to completely cool, add 2 chopped garlic cloves and 1 chopped hot chili pepper. Add mixture to quart jar containing kohlrabi and carrots. Place lid on jar and allow to sit at room temperature for 12 hours before eating. Keep refrigerated after a couple of days.

Note: This is a great side dish to add with rice, noodles, or in sandwiches. Almost everyone in Viet Nam uses white radishes instead of kohlrabi when preparing this dish, however my husband and I like kohlrabi's milder flavor. If you decide to try white radishes, know that extra steps need to be taken to remove their distinctively strong oder.

AROY-D
COCONUT MILK

Black Eyed Peas

SWEET RICE
SANPATONG
THREE RINGS
GLUTEN FREE

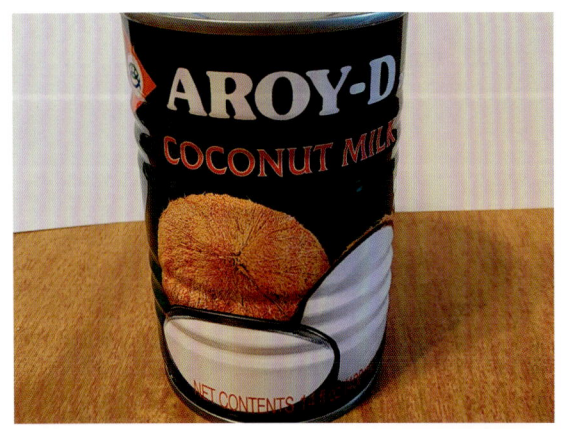

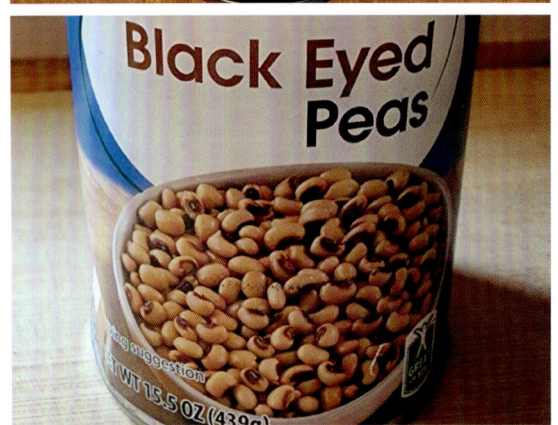

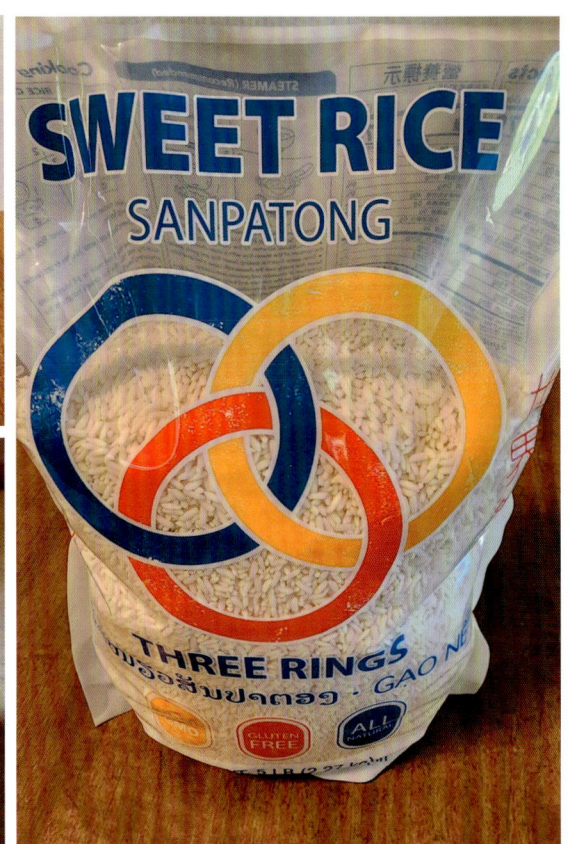

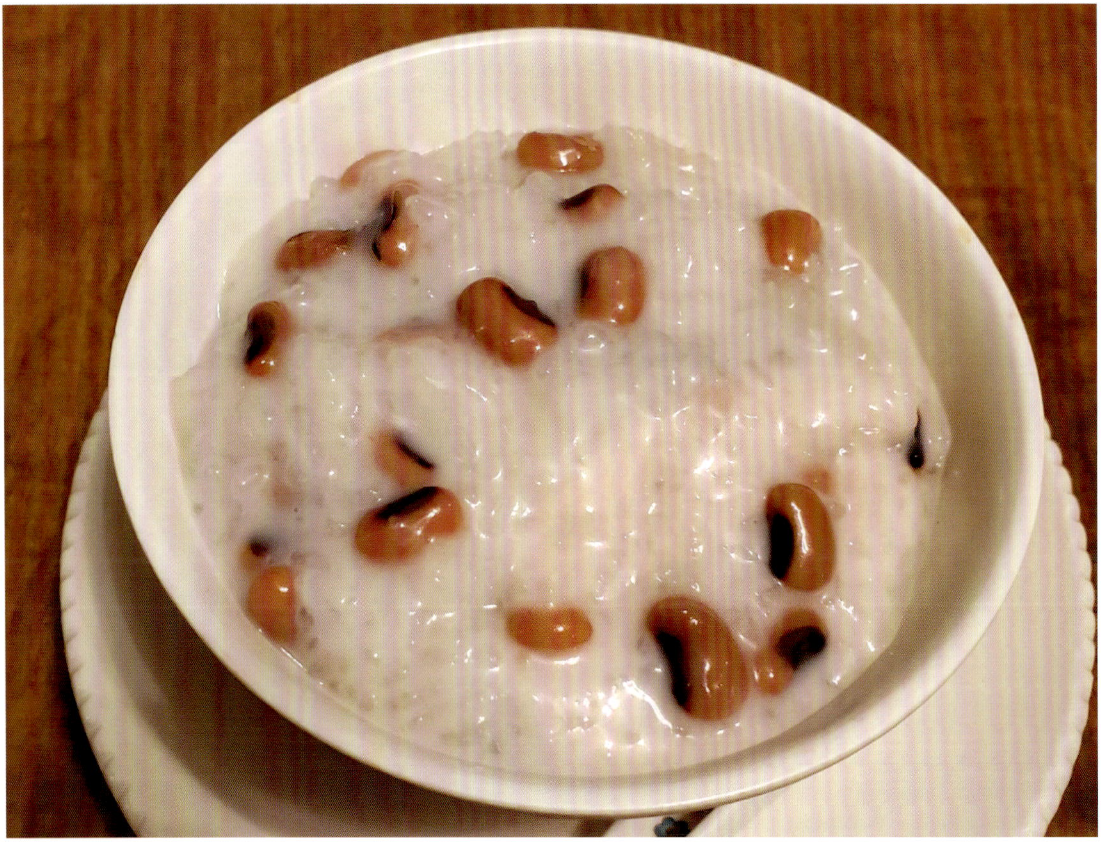

Vietnamese Sweet Rice & Bean Desert

- 1 cup of sweet rice (uncooked)
  (Also known as - sticky rice or Gao Nep)
- 1- 14 oz. can black-eyed peas
- 1 cup sugar
- 5 cups water
- 1- 13½ oz. can Coconut Milk
- Corn starch

1. In 4 quart non-stick sauce pan, add 1 cup of sweet rice, rinse 2-3 times to clean, then add 5 cups water. Allow to sit for 20 minutes.

2. Lightly rinse black-eye peas after opening if you prefer rice to remain white. Juices in can will create a slightly brown color. Set aside.

3. After sweet rice soaks for 20 minutes, place rice over heat. Bring to boil then simmer for 10 minutes while occasionally stirring, using care rice doesn't stick to the bottom or sides of pan. Remove from heat.

4. Add 1 cup sugar, black-eyed peas, and ⅔ of can of coconut milk. Place sauce pan back over heat and bring to a boil. Simmer over low heat for 5 minutes while stirring often.

5. Add 1½ tablespoons corn starch into remaining ⅓ can coconut milk, mix well and set aside.

6. Slowly add remaining coconut milk/corn starch mix while constantly stirring, making sure to go all around the edge and bottom of pan. Simmer for 2 more minutes while keeping in mind desert will become thicker when it cools. Remove from heat and allow to sit for 30 minutes before serving.

Delicious eaten warm or cold.

Mung Beans

Sweet Rice With Mung Bean

2 cups sweet rice
Salt
Coconut milk
¾ cup Mung bean
Sugar
⅓ cup crushed cashew nuts
Olive oil
2 Green onions (chopped)

1. In small bowl, add ⅓ cup crushed cashews, 2 tablespoons sugar, and ½ teaspoon salt. Mix well, set aside.

2. In rice cooker pan, add 2 cups sweet rice, cover with warm water for 30 minutes. Rinse well, then add 1 cup water and ¼ teaspoon salt. Place in rice cooker. When rice cooker switches back to warming, allow to rest 15 minutes. Add ½ cup coconut milk and stir until mixed. Allow to rest for 30 minutes or longer. Leftover coconut milk can be frozen for later use.

3. In medium size sauce pan, add ¾ cup mung beans and cover with warm water for 1 hour. Rinse well, then add 1¾ cups of water. Place over medium heat, bring to a boil and remove any scum that comes to the top. Cook on a low boil for 10 minutes or until water is mostly gone. Remove from heat.

4. Add 1½ teaspoons sugar and ½ teaspoon salt. Place over low heat, stir and press constantly for 2-3 minutes or until beans reach the texture of mashed potatoes. Remove from heat, cover with lid and allow to sit for 5 minutes.

5. In small skillet, add 1½ teaspoons olive oil and place over medium heat. When oil is hot, add 2 chopped green onions. Stir for 30-60 seconds or until white pieces of onion begin to brown. Remove from heat and add to mashed mung beans. Mix well.

6. In a 9x13 cake pan, add cooked sweet rice and spread evenly over pan bottom. Add mashed mung beans and spread evenly on top of sweet rice. Evenly sprinkle cashew mix over mung beans and allow to cool before cutting.

For a really special treat, top this dish off with "Vietnamese Sweet Rice & Bean Desert" (page 65)

Serves 10-12

About the Author

Trang Moreland grew up in Viet Nam. At the age 21, she immigrated to the United States. After overcoming language and cultural barriers, she was able to finish trade school and become a successful business owner. Her present business is Trang's Rentals.

Trang is currently Vice President of the Tuscarawas County Writers' Guild, an inspirational speaker and author of two books: "Just Smile and Say Hello" a true story about her life journey, and this cookbook, "I Am You".

Trang and her husband Jay live in Ohio and have two adult children. She donates to many local benefits and charities and provides school supplies for children in her native country.

Website: authortrangmoreland.com

Email: trangmmoreland@gmail.com

Follow Trang Moreland-Author on

Instagram: morelandtrang

Recipe Feedback

Absolutely delicious! Trang's recipes are some of the most flavorful and comforting foods I have had the pleasure of eating. You can tell she puts her heart into each dish.
Ashley S.

Over the past few months, Trang has treated the library staff to food from her cookbook. And what a treat it is! Everything from Trang's kitchen has been so tasty. Watching her husband Jay cook on FB inspires me to bring the flavors of Trang's homeland into my home. I can't wait to get my hands on that new cookbook and try every recipe! Congrats to my friend Trang on her new cookbook. I am sure it will be a big hit!
Sherrel R.

Trang's cooking is definitely restaurant quality and a unique style of home cooking. A pleasant experience for all taste buds. Being packed full of delicious flavor, these recipes are sure to be delightful addition to your meal rotation. Challenge yourself in the kitchen to try something new and you're sure to be pleased with the results.
Amanda M.

Recipe Feedback (cont.)

"Trang's dishes bring me so much joy. Not only is her food absolutely delicious, but it is incredibly fresh and nutritious. I love that her recipes can be sourced locally, which makes cooking more practical and easier on the wallet."

                                        Jim G.

Ok so lets be brutally honest here. Trang's food is freaking Amazing! The egg rolls are my favorite thing she has EVER made. Warm or cold they are fantastic! I recently tried her chicken curry and lets just say there was NOTHING left over! My kids even loved it, and I have 2 very picky eaters. I cannot wait to try more from this book! The flavors are out of this world and now I'm seeing why everyone has continued to ask for recipes from her restaurant owning days.

                                        Karryn H.

Trang has shared some of her recipes with me and every dish I've tried so far has been amazing. Her husband Jay did a great job organizing this cookbook, making it so simple to follow. I hope you will enjoy it as much as I'm going to.

                                        Cindy R.

The dishes in this book are hearty, comforting and delicious.

                                        Mallory T.

Family Recipe

Recipe Name -

Ingredients

Recipe Name -

Ingredients

Family Recipe

Recipe Name -

Ingredients

Recipe Name -

Ingredients

Family Recipe

Recipe Name -

Ingredients